SEA FISHING
PROPERLY EXPLAINED

In the same series, all uniform with this book

Begin Fishing The Right Way*
Secrets Of Fly-Fishing For Trout*
Freshwater Fishing Properly Explained*
The Knot Book

*By the same author

SEA FISHING PROPERLY EXPLAINED

Ian Ball

RIGHT WAY

CONTENTS

CHAPTER   PAGE

1   Reel Screamers!   7

2   Sure way to catch fish.   9

3   Get fish wise – know your fish!   15

Angler fish, 16; Bass, 17; Bream, black, 19; Bream, red, 21; Brill, 22; Coalfish, 23; Cod, 25; Conger eel, 26; Dab, 29; Dogfish (Smoothhound, 30; Starry smoothhound, 31; Bull huss, 32; Lesser spotted dogfish, 32; Spurdog, 32); Flounder, 34; Garfish, 36; Gurnard, yellow, 38; (Grey gurnard, 38; red gurnard, 38); Haddock, 39; Halibut, 40; John dory, 42; Ling, 44; Mackerel, 45; Mullet, thick-lipped, 46; (Thin-lipped mullet, 46; Golden grey mullet, 47); Plaice, 49; Pollack, 50; Pouting, 52; Ray, sting, 53; Ray, thornback, 54; (Small-eyed ray, 54); Skate, common, 56; Sole, 57; Tope, 58; Turbot, 59; Weever, greater, 61; (Lesser weever, 62); Whiting, 62; Wrasse, ballan, 64; (Cuckoo wrasse, 64).

4   Quality tackle for that perfect edge.   66

5   Best baits for bites.   71

6   Better safe than dead.   84

7   Estuary and harbour success secrets.   86

8   Champion beach casting.   89

9   Pier into yon distance.   94

10   Fishing on the rocks.   98

11   Ace boat fishing.   102

12   Knots, rigs and fishing methods.   105

13   Cook your catch.   123

     Index   125

1

REEL SCREAMERS!

Oceans and seas cover 71% of the world's surface. Vast areas of the sea have yet to be explored; its mysterious depths hide many unfamiliar species of fish.

When sea fishing we're never quite sure what we might catch!

Each of us lives within easy travelling distance of the sea; no costly rod licence or permit is required to begin fishing, and there's no close season. You may choose to fish from beach, rock outcrop, river estuary, pier, harbour wall or boat.

Sea fishing is a healthy, popular and fast-growing sport that offers thrilling pursuit of big fish, most of which provide a satisfying and nutritionally excellent meal later.

You can fill the freezer with fish fillets and cutlets, and regularly enjoy economical fish dishes that more than repay the price of tackle, bait and travel.

Should you wisely decide to join a sea fishing club, you'll benefit from the friendly, happy and helpful atmosphere; expert instruction and advice, plus valuable discounts on equipment and organised shore and boat fishing expeditions.

Reel screamers
Some giant fish will strip line from your reel and make it scream with strain. Conger eels, halibut and skate grow scaringly huge; sometimes large sharks come close inshore.

When you hook a sea fish, you're never certain what's on the other end of the line. In 1938 fishermen in the Indian Ocean caught a 2m (6 ft) coelacanth (Latimeria chalumnae) of the family Latimeriidae – thought to have been extinct for at least 60 million years. The coelacanth family was widespread in our oceans 350 million years ago – about 200 million years before dinosaurs roamed the earth!

Since the first coelacanth was captured and recognised, several more have been caught off the Comoro Islands in the Mozambique Channel, where the islanders, unaware of the fish's supposed extinction, had long regarded it as a tasty food dish.

And what of legendary sea monsters like the Norwegian "Kraken", and the Biblical "Leviathan". Do they exist? Now, they would be real, reel screamers!

2

SURE WAY TO CATCH FISH

The sure way of catching fish is to *know* which *species of fish* frequent the area of coast you anticipate fishing, and then scheme *the right way* to catch them.

There's no substitute for *local knowledge*. Visit local specialist tackle shops; talk with staff – buy a few items of necessary tackle and/or bait in exchange for their valuable and expert advice. Read the latest local "hotspots" sea angling news in angling newspapers and magazines. Chat to "locals" angling near spots you intend fishing; find out the fish species currently feeding along the coast; their favourite foods and baits. Then refer to the relevant Chapters in this book and *plan* your fishing expedition.

Care and attention to detail bring success

TIPS
1. Concentrate on one small stretch of coast; learn its secrets, then move on. Keep written records of your discoveries – after a few seasons your records will be worth their weight in gold!
2. In popular holiday months, a courteous 'phone call to the local tourist information centre often brings up-to-the-minute intelligence on sea fishing prospects.

TIDES
A tide is the action of rise and fall in sea level, influenced by the gravitational "pulling" power of the moon and to a lesser degree, the sun.

Along most areas of coastline, the tide rises and falls *twice* each day. So we should expect 2 high tides and 2 low tides in a period of 24 hours.

About *every two weeks* throughout the year, at new and full moon, sun and moon are in line with the earth, and exert enormous pulling power on the sea, causing high *spring tides*. The strongest seabed-churning storms usually occur during spring tides.

The highest spring tides rise at spring (21st March) and autumn (21st September) equinoxes. During all spring tides, the sea not only rises to a very high level, but also falls to a specially low level.

In the weeks between spring tides, smaller tides (rising and falling to a lesser extent) prevail; these smaller tides are called *neap tides*.

Around many coastal areas, the rising (flood) tide takes about 6 hours to reach its high tide level, and 6 hours to fall (ebb) to its low tide level. The period when the tide has reached and briefly settled at its high point, is commonly called "slack water". The term "slack water" is occasionally also used to mean the briefly settled state of the sea at low tide. In essence, "slack water" simply means still, unmoving water.

Tides, listed from high to low level:
HIGH WATER SPRING (HWS).
HIGH WATER NEAP (HWN).
LOW WATER NEAP (LWN).
LOW WATER SPRING (LWS).

The precise times of tides vary from place to place around the coast, and become a little later every day. Times of tides (tidal constants) are published for all areas in national angling newspapers and sea angling magazines.

TIPS
1. Low water spring (LWS) tide is an ideal opportunity to explore the seabed and chart in your records the promising patches to fish (see Chapters 7 to 11) at high tide.
2. Gathering natural baits (see Ch 5 page 71) is best carried out at low water spring (LWS) tide or low water neap (LWN)

tide.

3. High water spring (HWS) tide carries snooping fish close inshore, grubbing food previously hidden from them.

4. Admiralty charts, available for reference in some public reference libraries, or purchase to order from specialist tackle shops and bookshops, show water depths, seabed types (sand, reefs, rocks etc.) and contours, including the position of known wrecks!

WHERE, WHEN, WHY?

Fish shoals generally follow regular routes to feeding and breeding grounds at customary and predictable times of year; but routes and timing are subject to change, and may be altered owing to such factors as: cliff erosion and deviation of currents; exhaustion or disappearance of food sources; fluctuation of weather conditions and/or water temperature; presence of trawlers, pollution, noise etc. We must constantly update our records.

Fish choose to stay awhile in an area because: there's plenty of food; it's got convenient hang-outs to lurk in ambush, or hide from attack, like rocks and reefs, weeds, wrecks and/or sunken debris, breakwaters, pier or jetty supports, cracked stone harbour walls etc.

TIPS

1. Fish will be found near areas of seabed offering food and security.

2. Never rely on fish behaving *exactly* as they're supposed to behave according to books. The fish haven't read the books! If fish *have* read *this* book, they didn't pay for it!!

WATCH THE BIRDIE

Some birds are accomplished fishers. Watch for them and know where fish can be caught! Herons are partial to estuary flounders and freshwater eels; cormorants and gannets greedily devour mackerel, sandeels, flounders, and wrasse; gulls and terns snatch whole small shoal fish and the floating remains of fish shredded by hunting packs of bass or mackerel. Big predatory fish are seldom far from shoals of small fish.

1. The Black-Backed Gull

TIP
Spot a bird to find the fish!

GROUNDBAITING

Whether fishing from harbour wall, pier or jetty, rock outcrop, estuary or boat – groundbaiting helps hook fish!

You'll need some freshly caught fish (mackerel, herrings, sprats and pilchards are best); shellfish (optional) like limpets, mussels, cockles etc.; also bran and/or angler's fish meal, and angler's pilchard oil.

A tough, medium or "small" sized fine-meshed net bag (weighed with a few stones, if necessary) is filled with delicious titbits – chopped and diced fish; crushed shellfish; bran and/or fish meal – topped with piquant pilchard oil. The net bag is bunched tight at the top; tied shut with string; knotted to the end of a length of strong cord, and lowered into the water to rest about 1.21 m (4 ft) from your baited hook.

The groundbait bag *attracts feeding fish* to your hookbait. Jiggle the bag now and again to release minute juicy morsels into the current. Fish track the glorious scent for many metres!

Fishes' favourite groundbait dinner consists of about 85% chopped fish (or 70% chopped fish and 15% crushed shellfish) plus about 15% bran and/or angler's fish meal, laced with a liberal lashing of appetizing pilchard oil.

Prepare at least 680 g (1½ lbs) for use in your fine-meshed net bag. Estuary, harbour and rock anglers sometimes find (small approximately golf-ball sized) balls of the groundbait mixture, scattered 3 to 5 at a time onto the water above the hookbait at 15 to 25 minute intervals, more convenient and successful than the net bag. When using the scattered groundbait technique, add a few chopped samples of your hookbait for bonus results!

DETECTING BITES

Keep your rod tip high and the line tight. Hold the line near your reel gently between thumb and forefinger. When a fish bites the baited hook, you'll feel slight vibrations or tremors run up the line. With experience, you'll be able to identify the species of fish biting from the distinctive "feel" as it mouths the bait. Different species of fish investigate and seize food in their own unique way. Your rod tip will tremble, waver and may swing down sharply. If the rod bends double you've hooked a biggie!

Floats indicate a bite by wobbling, dipping, diving, disappearing, or speeding across the surface in suspicious fashion and/or against the current.

Immediately you detect a bite, *tighten your line* and reel-in!

TIP

Check you've packed *all* your tackle before travelling home!

CONSERVATION

Fish shoals fight for survival against natural predators *and* trawlers; and sea anglers.

Please help conserve declining fish stocks by returning small fishes, and fish not wanted for freezing and cooking (see Ch 13), *alive* to the sea. Thank you.

3

GET FISH WISE –
KNOW YOUR FISH!

Over 350 different species of sea fish swim in the coastal waters round Britain, Northern Ireland and Eire. Many of the fish popularly sought after, or encountered by sea anglers, are discussed in this Chapter, which reveals the essential facts necessary to begin catching the species of fish of your choice.

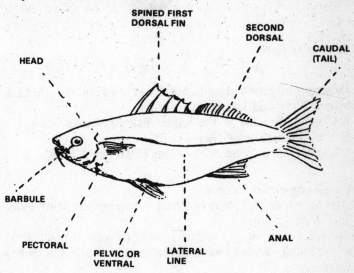

2. General features of sea fish

A clear understanding of fish behaviour helps us discover the best fishing methods. Get "fish wise"; know the right way to catch big fishes, and enjoy consistent sea angling success!

ANGLER FISH *(Lophius piscatorius).*
Family: Lophiidae
Average weight: Big rod-caught angler fish can weigh
27.21 Kg (60 lbs) or above. The average angler fish weighs
about 9.07 Kg (20 lbs).

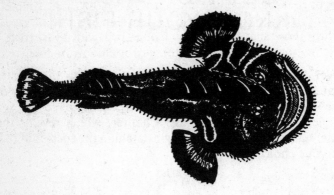

3. Angler Fish

Description: Easily identifiable. Huge head and mouth; dark
brown body and large pectoral fins.
WARNING: Beware of the angler fish's powerful jaws. It's
earned the nickname "Sea Devil"!
* Angler fish may be cooked and eaten (see Ch 13).

Catch angler fish! Hints:
Best locations: All parts of Britain, notably the south coast
and West Country.
Season: Summer visitor. MAY/JUNE/JULY/AUGUST/
SEPTEMBER. Withdraws to ocean depths at onset of wintry
weather.
Favourite feeding places: Prefers mud, sand, rocks and
wrecks lying under deep water – about 40 fathoms (73.15 m).
Sometimes comes into shallower inshore waters.
Successful baits: Any whole fresh fish, or generous fish strips
(mackerel, herring, pollack, pouting, and whiting are
recommended).

Right methods and rigs include:
Shore fishing: Basic leger (see rig, page 114) with a wire trace (see page 120) attaching hook to swivel on line; cast from beach, or rocks into deep water.
Boat fishing: Boat leger (see rig, page 118) with a wire trace (see page 120) attaching hook to swivel on line; simple paternoster (see rig, page 115) where bait is to be offered slightly above snag-ridden stretch of seabed, with a wire trace attaching hook to swivel on line, or rotten bottom (see rig, page 119) with a wire trace attaching hook to swivel on line.

EXPERT TIPS
1. Angler fish love rooting themselves in mud or sand; change colour to match their surroundings, and lure shoals of inquisitive fish by flicking and bobbing the rod-like spine of the dorsal fin above their cavernous mouths. Then they strike! The angler fish seldom pursues a moving bait and rarely rises far above the seabed to swallow food – so fish your bait on, or close to, the seabed.
2. Be alert. The angler fish removes bait from hooks with ease. Feel for faint knocks or tugs and tighten your line quickly.

BASS *(Dicentrachus labrax).*
Family: Serrandiae.
Average weight: Big rod-caught bass can weigh 6.35 Kg (14 lbs) or above. The average bass weighs about 2.26 Kg (5 lbs).

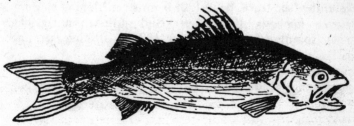

4. Bass

Description: Silvery sides; blue-grey back; cream – white belly. Two separate fins; the first with 9 spines; the second with 13. Large mouth – sharp teeth! WARNING: Watch for the dorsal spines; keep hands clear.

*** Bass are good to eat (see Ch 13).

Catch bass! Hints:

Best locations: Mainly south and south-west coasts of Britain, and southern Eire.

Season: All year. Best results in MAY/JUNE/JULY/AUGUST/ SEPTEMBER/OCTOBER. Many big bass migrate near November to deeper southern waters; returning about May/June.

Favourite feeding places: Rough, turbulent inshore waters; off rocky shorelines; over reefs and in fast tidal currents ripping along sandy shores. Also river estuaries; harbours and frequently many metres up tidal "freshwater" rivers.

Successful baits: Almost anything! Whole small fresh fish (sprats) or fish strips (mackerel, herring, squid); sandeels; shrimps; hermit crab (claws removed); crabs (peeler or soft back); prawns; shellfish; ragworms and lugworms (especially after dark).

Artificial baits; rubber or plastic sandeels; spoons; plugs and devon minnows; specially-tied flies or salmon or large trout flies (in river estuary or harbour waters, using freshwater fly fishing tackle and techniques).

Right methods and rigs include:

Shore fishing: Running paternoster (see rig, page 115); 2 hook running leger (see rig, page 117) cast from beach; spinning (see trace, page 120) from steep sloping shore.

Rocks, harbour, pier or jetty: Sliding float (see rig, page 111); spinning (see trace, page 120); driftlining (see page 121).

Boat fishing: Sliding float (see rig, page 111); boat leger (see rig, page 118); driftlining (see page 121); trolling (see page 122).

EXPERT TIPS

1. In estuaries and harbours, look for bass cruising near the surface.

2. At sea, watch for gulls, gannets or terns feeding on torn fish leavings; victims of large bass shoals.
3. Spot patches of water broken by shoals of terrified small fish herded to the surface by bass; to be attacked and eaten.
4. Don't cast too far! Bass often feed in shallow water close inshore. A long cast may overshoot hungry hunting bass.
5. Big bass feed at all depths; mid-water level is an ideal float setting when fishing from rocks.
6. To catch BIG bass, use a big bait!

BREAM, BLACK *(Spondyliosoma cantharus).*
Family: Sparidae.
Average weight: Big rod-caught black bream can weigh 2.26 Kg (5 lbs) or above. The average black bream weighs about 0.68 Kg (1½ lbs).

5. Black Bream

Description: Purple-grey back; silver-grey sides. Dark, broad vertical lines on sides. Dark spots on dorsal and anal fins. Ten or eleven sharp spines on dorsal fin. WARNING: Avoid dorsal spines when unhooking black bream.
*** Black bream are good to eat (see Ch 13).

Catch black bream! Hints:
Best locations: South coast of England, West Country and

Channel Islands. Sussex, and Littlehampton in particular, produces notable bream. Fine catches come also from the Isle of Wight; Hampshire and Dorset.

Season: Summer only visitor. MAY/JUNE/JULY/AUGUST/ SEPTEMBER. Black bream return to the Mediterranean when the weather (and water) turns cold.

Favourite feeding places: Deep water, about 10 fathoms (18.53 m) down, above weed covered rocks; although black bream do rise to feed near the surface when the tide is rushing in, or running out.

Successful baits: Fish strips (mackerel, pilchard and squid effective); ragworm, lugworm, shellfish, shrimps, small sandeels.

Right methods and rigs include:

Shore fishing: Basic leger (see rig, page 114) or running paternoster (see rig, page 115) from beach.

Rocks, pier or jetty: Sliding float (see rig, page 111) or driftlining (see page 121).

Boat fishing: Sliding float (see rig, page 111); boat leger (see rig, page 118); 2 hook paternoster (see rig, page 116), and driftlining (see page 121).

EXPERT TIPS

1. Groundbaiting (see page 13) is effective from rocks, piers, jetties or boats.

2. The black bream sucks food into its little and sensitive mouth, so use the smallest (and therefore least detectable) hook suited to the bait fished (see page 67).

3. Keep your bait on the move. Active baits excite black bream and invite attack. When fishing bait on the seabed, occasionally jerk and jiggle the line with your rod; raise the bait one or two metres and periodically wind bait, in stops and starts, to the surface. Black bream will follow and seize food near the top of the water.

BREAM, RED *(Pagellus bogaraveo).*
Family: Sparidae.
Average weight: Big rod-caught red bream can weigh
2.72 Kg (6 lbs) or above. The average red bream weighs
about 0.90 Kg (2 lbs).

6. Red Bream

Description: Crimson back, orange/gold sides, silvery-
orange underneath. Mature red bream have a distinctive
black patch at the beginning of the lateral line (see fig 2, page
15). Twelve sharp spines on dorsal fin. WARNING: Keep clear
of the dorsal spines.
*** Red bream are good to eat (see Ch 13).

Catch red bream! Hints:
Best locations: South and south west coasts of Britain;
particularly the West Country, also Eire.
Season: Summer visitor. MAY/JUNE/JULY/AUGUST/
SEPTEMBER.
Favourite feeding places: Deep water, about 12 fathoms
(21.94 m), over weed and rocks; can be caught in shallow
water, mainly after dark.
Successful baits: Shellfish, sandeels, whole small fish, or fish
strips; ragworm, lugworm etc. Eats almost anything that
looks and/or smells attractive and nourishing!

Right methods and rigs include:
Shore fishing: Basic leger (see rig, page 114) or running

paternoster (see rig, page 115) from beach.

Rocks, pier or jetty: Sliding float (see rig, page 111) or driftlining (see page 121).

Boat fishing: Sliding float (see rig, page 111); boat leger (see rig, page 118); 2 hook paternoster (see rig, page 116), and driftlining (see page 121).

EXPERT TIPS

1. A stationary bait fished on or near the seabed achieves best results during daytime.

2. Red bream feed prolifically after dark; often rising to the surface in search of food. Driftlining (see page 121) near the surface can prove a productive form of night fishing.

BRILL *(Scophthamlus rhombus).*
Family: Bothidae

Average weight: Big rod-caught brill can weigh 4.53 Kg (10 lbs) or above. The average brill weighs about 1.81 Kg (4 lbs).

Description: Closely resembles the turbot (see fig 27, page 60), speckled brown body on top; white underneath. Brill are frequently mistaken for turbot. However, the brill is less broad-bodied and more oval in outline than the turbot; brill – unlike turbot – have small scales on their bodies and none of the turbot's "tubercles" (see the turbot's description, page 59).

*** Brill are good to eat (see Ch 13).

Catch brill! Hints:

Best locations: All round British Isles and Eire; good catches of brill are taken off shores of southern Britain.

Season: Throughout the year; best in JUNE/JULY/AUGUST/ SEPTEMBER/OCTOBER/NOVEMBER/DECEMBER/JANUARY/ FEBRUARY.

Favourite feeding places: Offshore sand and sand/mud seabed beneath about 30 fathoms (54.86 m) of water; occasionally ventures closer inshore.

Successful baits: Whole live or freshly killed small fish (sprats, sandeels), or fish strips (mackerel); prawns, ragworms, lugworms.

Right methods and rigs include:
Shore fishing: Basic leger (see rig, page 114) cast into deep water.
Boat fishing: Boat leger (see rig, page 118).

***EXPERT TIP ***
1. When boat fishing for brill with leger rig, raise and lower your rod tip and / or reel-in, then unwind about 304 mm (1 ft) of line, at regular intervals – to lend attractive and extra-inviting movement to your bait.

COALFISH *(Pollachius virens).*
Family: Gadidae.
Average weight: Big rod-caught coalfish can weigh 8.16 Kg (18 lbs) or above. The average coalfish weighs about 3.17 Kg (7 lbs).

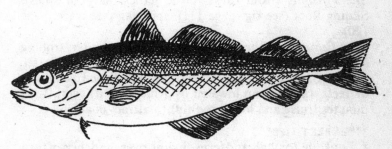

7. Coalfish

Description: Cousin to the cod. Young coalfish are called "billet". Coalfish are black on the back, have blue-green sides and a silver-grey belly. Nearly straight white-dashed lateral line (see fig 2, page 15). Lower jaw juts out just beyond upper jaw; there's a small barbule (feeler) on the coalfish's chin.
* Coalfish may be cooked and eaten (see Ch 13).

Catch coalfish! Hints:
Best locations: Rocky shores. Most common off coast of northern England, Scotland and Northern Ireland. Can be

caught in deep water above West Country rocks, reefs and wrecks.

Season: Throughout year. Best sport in MAY/JUNE/JULY/AUGUST/SEPTEMBER/OCTOBER/NOVEMBER.

Favourite feeding places: Weed-covered rocks; estuaries and harbours. Big coalfish feed in deep water over offshore reefs and wrecks, but return inshore when the weather turns cold. Coalfish feed near the seabed and at mid-water depth.

Successful baits: Any whole small fish, or fish strips (cod, mackerel, herring, squid, whiting); lugworms, ragworms, sandeel, shrimp, prawn.

Artificial baits: rubber or plastic sandeels; spoons; devon minnows; pirks; specially tied or salmon or large trout flies (in river estuary or harbour waters; from boats on a calm sea, using freshwater fly fishing tackle and techniques).

Right methods and rigs include:

Shore fishing (from rocks, piers, jetties, harbour walls): Sliding float (see rig, page 111); spinning (see trace, page 120).

Boat fishing: Driftlining (see page 121) deep water; trolling (see page 122); pirk "jigging" (see page 122); feathering (see page 121); rotten bottom (see rig, page 119) fished over rocks or reefs – raised and lowered by 1 metre (3 ft) every 3 – 5 minutes (raise and lower rod tip) to attract coalfish.

EXPERT TIPS

1. Look out for gulls and terns circling over the debris of torn floating fish marking the position of a shoal of feeding coalfish.

2. When float fishing without success, a slow "jerky" rewinding of line may tempt tardy coalfish to take your bait.

3. Big coalfish hunt food away from large shoals of smaller coalfish, and prefer whole fish or fish strip baits, especially herring and small cod.

4. Boat fishing in deep water over rocks; first offer your bait about 1 metre (3 ft) above the rocks. If you haven't caught a coalfish after 20 minutes, raise your bait a further 1 metre (3 ft) and so on . . . until you contact a feeding coalfish shoal.

5. Keep hooked coalfish away from rocks and/or submerged snags and obstructions. Draw coalfish quickly to the surface on a tight line.

6. Coalfish often rise to feed near the surface at dawn and dusk.

COD *(Gadus morhua).*
Family: Gadidae.
Average weight: Big rod-caught cod can weigh 14.5 Kg (32 lbs) or above. The average cod weighs about 5.44 Kg (12 lbs).

8. Cod

Description: Big head; bulky, brown-green or olive-green body. Large mouth, bedded with small sharp teeth; barbule (feeler) below chin.

*** Cod are good to eat (see Ch 13).

Catch cod! Hints:
Best locations: All round British Isles, particularly northern and eastern waters. Some good boat fishing for BIG cod in West Country waters above sunken ship wrecks, and around Isle of Wight in Hampshire.

Season: Autumn and winter visitor to many coastal areas of Britain and Eire; though can be caught off Scottish coast throughout the year. Cod may be caught in northern waters from JUNE to MARCH; cod shoals arrive off the south coast round OCTOBER and melt away about FEBRUARY.

Favourite feeding places: Prefer deep water; scour the seabed for food. Cod shoals rove remorselessly in search of rich feeding grounds; consume everything edible – then move on.

Successful baits: Almost anything! Cod snatch and digest all natural baits: whole fish or fish strips; lugworms, ragworms, sandeels, shellfish, crabs etc.

Right methods and rigs include:
Shore fishing: Basic leger (see rig, page 114); simple paternoster (see rig, page 115) cast into deep water.
Boat fishing: Boat leger (see rig, page 118); driftline (see page 121) fished deep; trolling (see page 122); feathering (see page 121); jigging (see page 122).

EXPERT TIPS
1. Big cod feed enthusiastically when the tide is changing; either ebbing (flowing out) or flooding (rushing in). Cod are most active in their search for food when the sea is rough.
2. Watch for gulls diving at shoals of sprat; cod won't be far away!
3. Don't be afraid to fish a large bait for cod. A 4.5 Kg (10 lb) cod can swallow a 1 Kg (2¼ lbs) whole fish AND a few sprats as an appetizer before the main meal!
4. Some boat anglers, fishing for big cod, like to attach a wire trace (see page 120) of about 11.33 Kg (25 lbs) breaking strain between hook and swivel on line.

CONGER EEL *(Conger conger).*
Family: Congridae.
Average weight: Big rod-caught conger eels can weigh 27.21 Kg (60 lbs) or above. Commercial fishermen have reported catching conger eels of approximately 100 Kg (220 lbs) in weight. Such monsters have also been sighted by deep-sea divers. The average rod-caught conger eel weighs about 9.07 Kg (20 lbs).

Description: Serpent-like head; wide protruding eyes; slime-covered scaleless body; powerful jaws and razor-sharp teeth!
WARNING: Dodge those teeth!!
*** Conger eels are good to eat (see Ch 13).

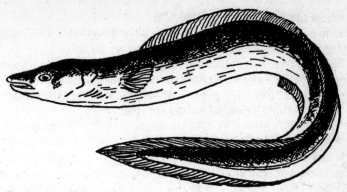

9. Conger Eel

Catch conger eels! Hints:
Best locations: All round British Isles; Northern Ireland and Eire.
Season: All year; inshore conger eels are more responsive to bait offered in warm weather. During very cold winter weather, some conger eels withdraw to deep offshore hideaways, returning about MAY. The *monster* deep water conger eels live in a world of perpetual cold and dark, and strike at bait in all seasons; day or night! The most profitable months to fish for big inshore conger eels are JUNE/JULY/AUGUST/SEPTEMBER/OCTOBER.
Favourite feeding places: Conger eels live in rocky crevices, holes, hollows, caverns and sunken wrecks; by harbour walls, breakwaters and underneath piers and jetties. Conger eels set up home and stay put! Unless extremely cold conditions drive them temporarily into deeper water, or they outgrow their lair and must move somewhere more spacious. Conger eels seldom stray far from the safety of their hideouts and prey on passing fish.
Successful baits: Whole *live* fish, hooked through the upper jaw behind the lip (mackerel, pouting, whiting) or whole freshly killed fish (squid, herring, bunch of sprats or pilchards); ½ fresh fish (top and bottom halves effective); or occasionally fish strips – large helpings preferred! Also crabs and lobsters.

Right methods and rigs include:

Shore fishing: Basic leger (see rig, page 114) with a wire trace (see page 120) attaching hook to swivel on line.

Boat fishing: Boat leger (see rig, page 118) with a wire trace (see page 120) attaching hook to swivel on main line; running paternoster (see rig, page 115) with a wire trace (see page 120) attaching hook to swivel on line.

EXPERT TIPS

1. Big conger eels lurk in some pretty obvious places close inshore, and in "shallow" water not more than 2 fathoms (3.7m) deep! Because inshore conger eels stay hidden 'til night, their presence is often unsuspected. Look for likely lairs – sunken boat hulls, broken pipes, dumped scrap, old collapsing jetties, cracked or holed harbour walls, narrow underwater clefts in rock outcrops etc.

2. Herring, mackerel, sprat and pilchard make good bait because their high oil content lays a scent trail which conger eels quickly detect and find irresistible.

3. Conger eels respond to groundbaiting (see page 13). In deep offshore water, weight a large and strong brown paper bag (or 2 strong brown paper bags, one inside the other, for extra strength) with a few heavy stones; top up with conger's favourite goodies – fresh fish blood and guts, mixed with bran soaked in cod liver oil or angler's pilchard oil; bunch the bag tight shut; fasten round with fishing line or wire, and heave into the sea. The bag breaks open on hitting the seabed and the conger eel community thinks it's Christmas! Conger eels live alone, but belong to small sociable groups; so where there's one big conger eel, other members of the conger's clique won't be far away!

4. The tingling feel in the air on hot, humid evenings shortly before a thunderstorm breaks, electrifies conger eels into a feeding frenzy; they frequently snatch baits in suicidal haste.

5. Conger eels normally play cat and mouse with baits before gulping them down. Don't reel-in line at the first tug; wait until line strips off your reel and the running conger's bending your rod – then recover the line and begin fighting the conger eel to the surface. Immediately you apply pressure, the conger eel knows it's hooked and dives towards obstacles around which to wrap and snap your line. Don't let this happen – maintain pressure and pump the eel upwards through the water by lowering your rod; reeling-in line; raising the rod, then lowering, smartly reeling-in and so on...

6. Manoeuvre the landed conger eel straightaway into an old sack; cut line (or unclip, if using a link swivel attachment). Should you intend keeping the conger for cooking, tie sack top with string; store away from easy reach of the sea. Conger eels may be stunned by a blow from a heavy object to the head, but can only be killed by severing the spine with a sharp knife or striking the head off with an axe. Neither method of execution ought to be risked in a small boat or on slippery rocks – wait until you're safely ashore. And don't be fooled by congers playing "dead". Some survive out of water for *hours*!

DAB *(Limanda limanda).*
Family: Pleuronectidae.
Average weight: Big rod-caught dabs can weigh 0.68 Kg (1½ lbs) or above. The average dab weighs about 340 g (12 oz.)

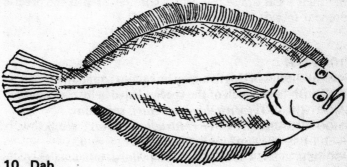

10. Dab

Description: Rounded, thin body. Sandy-brown back (sometimes with dark spots), white underneath.
*** Dabs are good to eat (see Ch 13).

Catch dabs! Hints:
Best locations: Found along sandy estuaries and shallow water close inshore. Dabs don't dwell round really rocky coastlines; otherwise common to Britain and Eire. Adult dabs move into deeper offshore waters in spring/summer to spawn, and head out to sea in severe wintry weather.
Season: Small dabs can be caught close inshore throughout the year; big dabs inshore (except during freezing weather): AUGUST / SEPTEMBER / OCTOBER / NOVEMBER / DECEMBER / JANUARY/FEBRUARY; busy breeding and recovering offshore for remaining months.
Favourite feeding places: On the bottom of shallow sandy bays; sand/mud estuaries and sometimes many metres up river.
Successful baits: Small pieces of fish; ragworm, lugworm, cockles, hermit crabs, sandeels, peeled shrimps, razorfish.

Right methods and rigs include:
Shore fishing and *boat fishing:* Basic leger (see rig, page 114); 2 hook paternoster (see rig, page 116).

EXPERT TIP
1. Dab shoals seek food in the same spots at regular times; so find their local time-table and accurately predict the precise moment to cast out and pull dabs in!

DOGFISH
Several species of dogfish may be caught round the shores of the British Isles. Each of the species listed below is a dogfish:
SMOOTHHOUND *(Mustelus mustelus)*, see below.
SMOOTHHOUND, STARRY *(Mustelus asterias)*, see below.
BULL HUSS *(Scyliorhinus stellaris)*, see page 32.
DOGFISH, LESSER SPOTTED *(Scyliorhinus canicula)*, see page 32.
SPURDOG *(Squalus acanthias)*, see page 32.
  Dogfish are closely related to the tope (see page 58) and *sharks*!
SMOOTHHOUND *(Mustelus mustelus). Family: Triakidae.*

SMOOTHHOUND, STARRY *(Mustelus asterias). Family: Triakidae.*

Average weight: Big rod-caught Smoothhounds and Starry Smoothhounds can weigh 9.07 Kg (20 lbs) or above. The average Smoothhound and Starry Smoothhound weigh about 4.53 Kg (10 lbs).

Description: The Smoothhound closely resembles the tope, and is often mistaken for tope (see fig 26, page 58). The Smoothhound is slightly less streamlined in appearance than the tope; the Smoothhound's first dorsal fin is positioned further forward, closer to its head, and the Smoothhound's teeth are short close-set, slab-like grinders; the tope has long and sharp, flesh-tearing teeth.

The Smoothhound has a grey back; light grey sides and white belly.

The Starry Smoothhound is of similar shape to the smoothhound, but its grey body is dotted with white spots or "stars".

NOTE: Both smoothhound and starry smoothhound may be caught using similar methods, rigs and baits; in the following notes both species will be referred to simply as "smooth-hounds".

*** Smoothhounds are good to eat (see Ch 13).

Catch smoothhounds! Hints:

Best locations: All round Britain; numerous along southern shores, especially the south-east.

Season: Summer; shoals of smoothhounds come close inshore in MAY; their feeding peaks in JUNE/JULY/AUGUST. Smoothhounds move into deeper offshore waters in SEPTEMBER/OCTOBER.

Favourite feeding places: Wide ranging. Smoothhounds patrol the seabed at offshore depths of about 60 fathoms (109.72 m); then steer inshore and cruise contentedly in 2 metres (6½ ft) of water. Smoothhounds enjoy hunting across areas of sand or sand/mud seabed.

Successful baits: Strips of fresh fish (mackerel, herring, squid); peeler and soft-backed crabs, ragworms, shellfish, prawns.

Right methods and rigs include:
Shore fishing: Basic leger (see rig, page 114); running paternoster (see rig, page 115).
Boat fishing: Boat leger (see rig, page 118); running paternoster (see rig, page 115).

EXPERT TIPS
1. Some sea anglers like to attach a wire trace (see page 120) of about 9.07 Kg (20 lbs) breaking strain between hook and swivel on line.
2. Smoothhounds feed voraciously on hot summer's evenings, as light begins to fade. Dawn may bring good catches.
3. Smoothhounds often play with food before eating it, so allow time for a toying smoothhound to finish its game before tightening your line. Begin reeling-in when the line moves out; pulls taut and starts bending your rod tip.
4. When you hook a smoothhound, land it quickly and cast for another. The shoal stay in one place for a short spell only; sometimes as little as 20 minutes, then move onwards. But during their brief visit, they mop up all appetizing food in sight!
5. Get to know the smoothhound shoal's patrol routes. The shoal sticks to regular routes and feeding times – until there's a sudden change in temperature, or a new patrol route is explored and adopted.

BULL HUSS *(Scyliorhinus stellaris). Family: Scyliorhinidae.*
DOGFISH, LESSER SPOTTED *(Scyliorhinus canicula). Family: Scyliorhinidae.*
SPURDOG *(Squalus acanthias). Family: Squalidae.*
Average weights: Big rod-caught bull huss can weigh 7.25 Kg (16 lbs) or above. The average bull huss weighs about 3.62 Kg (8 lbs).

Big rod-caught lesser spotted dogfish can weigh 1.59 Kg (3½ lbs) or above. The average lesser spotted dogfish weighs about 1 Kg (2¼ lbs).

Big rod-caught spurdogs can weigh 6.80 Kg (15 lbs) or

above. The average spurdog weighs about 3.17 Kg (7 lbs).
Descriptions: Both bull huss and lesser spotted dogfish are
of shark-like appearance; have a sand-brown or rust-brown
body, dotted with dark brown spots, and white belly. The
bull huss has one separate frilled flap of skin beneath each
nostril. The lesser spotted dogfish has a continuous,
unfrilled nasal flap between nostrils.

The spurdog is also of shark-like shape; blue-grey or
brown-grey body; smattering of light-grey/white spots on
sides.

WARNING: Bull huss and lesser spotted dogfish have sand-
paper rough skin – handle with care! Don't let these "dogs"
wrap their body around unprotected arms. A thick leather
glove or gauntlet provides welcome protection. Also
BEWARE of large bull huss' teeth!

Spurdogs have a sharp spine or "spur" at the front of each
of their two small dorsal fins. These two spurs can inflict
painful wounds!
*** Bull huss, lesser spotted dogfish and spurdogs are good
to eat (see Ch 13). These fish are sometimes marketed as
"huss" and "rock salmon".

NOTES
Bull huss are "loners"; they lie in offshore water over rough,
rocky ground. Bull huss are commonly caught during the
summer round southern Britain, but may be found all
around the British Isles, and in any season. Bull huss feed on
or near the seabed; their favourite food includes: crabs,
sandeels, ragworms, lugworms, whole small fish (sprats) or
fish strips (mackerel, whiting, pilchard, squid).

Bull huss habitually swim away with bait before biting and
getting hooked. Tighten your line firmly *twice* or *thrice* when
you judge you might have a bull huss on the other end of the
line.

Lesser spotted dogfish swim in shoals off all coastal areas
of Britain; found all year round – close inshore from JUNE to
OCTOBER. Lesser spotted dogfish prefer feeding over soft
(non-rocky) ground; taking baits fished near the surface, or
on the seabed. Successful baits include: strips of fresh fish
(mackerel, herring, pilchard) and whole fresh small fish.

Spurdogs hunt in packs along shores all around Britain; feed close inshore in summertime, and at varying depths. Spurdogs pursue shoals of small fish relentlessly. Spurdogs respond to almost any bait, especially strips of fresh fish and whole small fish.

Right methods and rigs include:
Bull huss, lesser spotted dogfish and spurdogs can be caught using similar methods and rigs to those recommended for smoothhounds (see page 32).

FLOUNDER *(Platichthys flesus).*
Family: Pleuronectidae.
Average weight: Big flounders can weigh 1.58 Kg (3½ lbs) or above. The average flounder weighs about 0.45 Kg (1 lb).

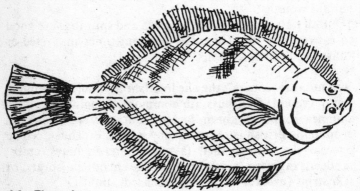

11. Flounder

Description: Dark green-brown back; pearl-white underside. Rows of small knobs or "tubercles" can be found where the lateral line meets the gill-cover. Flounders may be dark blotched top and bottom.
*** Flounders are good to eat (see Ch 13).

Catch flounders! Hints:
Best locations: All round British and Irish coasts.

Season: Throughout the year, though mature flounders move into deep offshore water to spawn mid-winter, and may be absent from shallow inshore waters for 3 – 4 months, usually JANUARY / FEBRUARY / MARCH or JANUARY/ FEBRUARY/ MARCH/APRIL. Naturally, flounders depart and return according to water temperature rather than calendar, and there can be variation in the months flounders spawn.

Favourite feeding places: On or near the bottom of sand and/or mud covered estuaries and harbours. Flounders are frequently found several kilometres up tidal rivers, often well into fresh water. Flounders also feed beneath piers and jetties.

Successful baits: Ragworm, lugworm, shellfish, fish strips (herring, mackerel, pilchard, sprat); shrimps, sandeels, hermit crab tail, peeler crabs, soft-backed crabs.

Artificial baits: flounder spoons (baited with a titbit of one of the above listed baits).

Right methods and rigs include:
Shore fishing: Basic leger (see rig, page 114); 2 hook paternoster (see rig, page 116); 3 hook paternoster (see rig, page 116); spinning (see trace, page 120); light float (see rig, page 111) or sliding float (see rig, page 111) set to present bait slightly above bottom in estuary and harbour waters.

Boat fishing: Boat leger (see rig, page 118); 2 hook running leger (see rig, page 117); 2 hook paternoster (see rig, page 116); trolling (see page 122).

EXPERT TIPS
1. Flounders follow the flood tide onto beaches and into estuaries to investigate disturbed sand and mud for lugworms, ragworms and any food on offer. Fish for flounders on a racing and rising tide for great results.

2. Flounders feed in extremely shallow water; sometimes sufficient only to cover their backs. Long distance casts into deep water are seldom necessary.

3. Pack all of a bait firmly onto the hook; flounders filch loosely fixed baits and flapping bits of bait clean away from the hook in a trice.

4. Reel in line regularly and re-cast to arouse interest of flounders, and check your bait is intact!

5. Flounders travel in mixed-size small shoals; moving with the current. One shoal follows another at intervals of up to about 137 m (150 yds). To track a particular shoal you've located, follow the current, making allowance for the flounder shoal's modest pace. If you lose a shoal, don't despair – there's another shoal behind!

6. Flounders continue to feed hungrily in the coldest wintry weather; so don't be deterred by frost on your ear lobes. The flounders are feeding!

GARFISH *(Belone belone).*
Family: Belonidae.
Average weight: Big rod-caught garfish can weigh 0.90 Kg (2 lbs) or above. The average garfish weighs about 454 g (1 lb).

12. Garfish

Description: Cross between an eel and a long-beaked bird! Blue-green body; silvery sides. The garfish's sword-like beak/mouth is equipped with rows of small sharp teeth, which might give a nasty nip – be careful! Related to the flying fish, garfish love leaping from the sea to turn aerial somersaults over the waves.

* Garfish may be cooked and eaten (see Ch 13).
Don't be put off by the appearance of its cooked green bones!

Catch garfish! Hints:

Best locations: Swims happily in most waters along Britain's coastline; caught mainly off southern shores of England and the West Country.

Season: Summer visitor. Arrives off British coast about MAY/JUNE, stays through JULY and AUGUST; disappears around SEPTEMBER/OCTOBER.

Favourite feeding places: Surface and mid-water level of any patch of sea holding small fish. Dives down towards seabed in rough and stormy weather. Cruises over wide areas of sea seeking food. Frequently found close inshore.

Successful baits: Small whole fish (sprats, sandeels, whitebait) or fish strips (mackerel, herring); lugworm, ragworm, prawns.

Artificial baits: spoons, devon minnows.

Right methods and rigs include:

Shore fishing: (rocks, pier, jetty, harbour wall): Light float (see rig, page 111); sliding float (see rig, page 111); spinning (see trace, page 120) also spinning from steep sloping beach.

Boat fishing: Light float (see rig, page 111); sliding float (see rig, page 111); spinning (see trace, page 120); driftlining (see page 121) near surface; trolling (see page 122).

EXPERT TIPS

1. Garfish are often found in the company of mackerel shoals.

2. Garfish respond to groundbaiting (see page 13).

3. Rapidly retrieved artificial spinning lures can be super-successful. The brighter your lure the better!

4. Tighten line on a garfish swimming away with your bait by sweeping your rod *sideways* (not straight up). A sideways action drives your hook securely into the side of the garfish's mouth. An upwards motion of the rod pulls your bait from its hard beak!

GURNARD, YELLOW *(Trigla lucerna)*. Also known as "Tubfish".
Family: Triglidae.
Average weight: Big rod-caught yellow gurnard can weigh 3.62 Kg (8 lbs) or above. The average yellow gurnard weighs about 1 Kg (2¼ lbs).

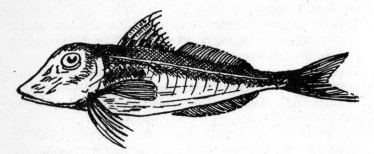

13. Gurnard

Description: Distinctive shape; glorious colour: deep red-orange/yellow; pectoral fins edged by bright blue bands.
Warning: The gurnard's spine ribbed fins can cut skin.
NOTE: Of similar shape is the GREY GURNARD (*Eutrigla gunardus*), average weight about 227 g (½ lb); purple-grey back. And the RED GURNARD (*Aspitrigla cuculus*), average weight about 454 g (1 lb); brilliant red body.

Yellow, grey and red gurnard may each be caught in similar locations, using identical methods, rigs and baits. The grey gurnard is the more common of the three; the yellow gurnard is generally the heaviest, and makes the most filling meal!
*** Gurnard are good to eat (see Ch 13).

Catch gurnard! Hints:
Best locations: Found round coasts of Britain, Northern Ireland and Eire.
Season: Gurnard come close inshore during the summer months, JUNE/JULY/AUGUST/SEPTEMBER and return to deeper offshore waters from OCTOBER to APRIL/MAY.

Favourite feeding places: On or near the bottom of soft sand or sand/mud areas of seabed between rocks and reefs; inshore and offshore.
Successful baits: Fish strips (herring, mackerel); sandeel, shrimps, crabs (soft-backed).

Right methods and rigs include:
Shore fishing: Basic leger (see rig, page 114); running paternoster (see rig, page 115).
Boat fishing: Boat leger, (see rig, page 118); simple paternoster (see rig, page 115).

HADDOCK *(Melanogrammus aeglefinus).*
Family: Gadidae.
Average weight: Big rod-caught haddock can weigh 3.62 Kg (8 lbs) or above. The average haddock weighs about 1 Kg (2¼ lbs).

14. Haddock

Description: Grey-brown/bronze back, shading into white belly. Black lateral line; black mark above each pectoral fin; small barbule (feeler) on chin. Related to the cod.

Haddock are good to eat. However, the species has become scarce around British shores due to past commercial over-fishing, and where possible captured haddock should be returned ALIVE to the sea.

Catch haddock! Hints:
Best locations: The haddock is now steadily re-establishing its numbers, and is most plentiful around the coasts of Scotland, north-eastern England, Northern Ireland, and deep water off the West Country.
Season: All year round, especially JUNE/JULY/AUGUST/ SEPTEMBER/OCTOBER/NOVEMBER/DECEMBER. Come close inshore during winter months.
Favourite feeding places: Haddock feed on or near the bottom of deep water off steep-sloping beaches or rocky outcrops. Haddock shoals sift sandy and soft sand/mud seabed areas for food.
Successful baits: Ragworm, lugworm; shellfish (mussels and cockles are haddock favourites); whole small fish (sprat, pilchard) or fish strips (mackerel, herring, squid); shrimps, crabs (soft-backed), starfish.

Right methods and rigs include:
Shore fishing: 2 boom paternoster (see rig, page 117); 2 hook paternoster (see rig, page 116); simple paternoster (see rig, page 115) – *cast into deep water.*
Boat fishing: Boat leger (see rig, page 118); 2 boom paternoster (see rig, page 117); 2 hook paternoster (see rig, page 116).

EXPERT TIPS
1. When boat fishing safely away from rocks and reefs, be prepared to move your boat in the same direction and at the same speed as feeding shoals of haddock you hook into; haddock shoals are constantly on the move, combing the seabed for food.
2. In water 20 fathoms (37 m) or more deep; adjust paternoster rigs to present one baited hook about 1 m (3 ft) above the seabed, and a second (if any) baited hook about 1.82 m (6 ft) above the seabed.

HALIBUT *(Hippoglossus hippoglossus).*
Family: Pleuronectidae.
Average weight: Big rod-caught halibut can weigh 40.82 Kg

(90 lbs) or above. Commercial deep sea trawlers have netted single halibut over 113.39 Kg (250 lbs) in weight. Halibut are believed to reach weights in excess of 317 Kg (700 lbs)! Fancy hooking one? The average rod-caught halibut weighs about 13.60 Kg (30 lbs).

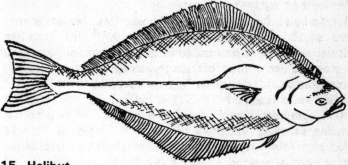

15. Halibut

Description: Dark olive-brown on top; white underside. Lateral line curves over pectoral fins. Strong jaws and sharp teeth! WARNING: Treat the halibut's mouth with the caution its teeth command.
*** Halibut are good to eat (see Ch 13).

Catch halibut! Hints:
Best locations: The deep, cold seas round northern Scotland; Orkneys; Shetland, and occasionally Northern Ireland.
Season: All year round. Best sport likely JULY/AUGUST/ SEPTEMBER/OCTOBER/NOVEMBER.
Favourite feeding places: Deep offshore waters. Halibut feed at depths ranging from 30 fathoms (54.86 m) and above to 600 fathoms (1,097 m) and below! Take plenty of line!
Successful baits: Whole live fish (coalfish, pollack, mackerel, haddock, whiting, squid); freshly killed whole fish, or fish strips.

Right methods and rigs include:
Boat fishing: Rotten bottom (see rig "A", page 119) over rocky ground, with a wire trace (see page 120) attaching hook to swivel on main reel line; or boat leger (see rig, page

118) with a wire trace (see page 120) attaching hook to swivel on main reel line; driftlining (see page 121) with a wire trace (see page 120) attaching hook to swivel on main reel line, fished deep – a few metres above the seabed.

EXPERT TIPS

1. Live bait is best (fish hooked through its upper jaw behind the lip). Put enticing movement into freshly killed whole fish or fish strips, by raising and lowering your rod and/or reel-in a metre or two of line, then slowly release the same length of line. Repeat this action at regular intervals.

2. If you're chasing MONSTER halibut, employ standard giant common skate or shark fishing tackle. You'll need a strong shoulder harness and rod-butt holder; at LEAST 365.76 m (400 yds) of 36.28 Kg (80 lbs) breaking strain line; wire trace of around 40.82 Kg (90 lbs) breaking strain and nerves of steel!

JOHN DORY *(Zeus faber).*
Family: Zeidae.
Average weight: Big rod-caught john dory can weigh 4 Kg (9 lbs) or above. The average john dory weighs about 0.90 Kg (2 lbs).

16. John Dory

Description: Brown-olive body: yellow-gold stripes and whisps. Black spot on each side – St. Peter's thumb prints, or so legend says. John dory is known as "St. Peter's fish". WARNING: Don't touch the sharp-spiked dorsal fin. Note where St. Peter (a professional fisherman) placed his thumbs, and do likewise, or you'll be sorry!
*** John dory are good to eat (see Ch 13).

Catch john dory! Hints:
Best locations: Inshore and deep offshore water – as far down as 110 fathoms (201 m). Caught mainly off West Country coastline; western Northern Ireland and Eire. Also found round shores of southern England.
Season: Throughout the year. Big john dory move from inshore to deep offshore water in cold and/or rough weather.
Favourite feeding places: Wherever shoals of small fish gather, there will be john dory. Near rocks and reefs; round wrecks; wherever fish make easy prey, there drifts john dory!
Successful baits: Small whole fish (herring, sprat, pilchard); fish strips (squid, herring, mackerel); prawns, shrimps, sandeels.

Right methods and rigs include:
Shore fishing: Simple paternoster (see rig, page 115) cast into deep water; running paternoster (see rig, page 115) cast into deep water.
Boat fishing: 2 hook paternoster (see rig, page 116); simple paternoster (see rig, page 115); driftlining (see page 121) at mid-water or deep water depth.

EXPERT TIPS
1. To catch fish for meals, john dory, who can't swim fast, drifts in harmless fashion towards unsuspecting victims; opens his mouth, and SUCKS them in! An anchored or slow moving bait is therefore most likely to succeed in arousing john dory's interest.
2. John dory feed largely on fish, preferably live; certainly fresh.
3. One of the best ways to bag dory is with paternostered live

sandeels; live prawns, or freshly killed sprats are also highly effective.

LING *(Molva molva).*
Family: Gadidae.
Average weight: Big rod-caught ling can weigh 18.14 Kg (40 lbs) or above. Commercial trawlers have netted specimens weighing in excess of 294 Kg (650 lbs)! The average ling weighs about 6.80 Kg (15 lbs).

17. Ling

Description: Back olive-brown/yellow. Body marbled yellow/gold-brown. White belly. Tail, dorsal and anal fins lined white along edges. Barbule (feeler) on lower jaw. WARNING: Ling are armed with strong teeth! Keep your finger away from the jaws.
*** Ling are good to eat (see Ch 13).

Catch ling! Hints:
Best locations: Found all round Britain. Noteworthy catches are made off the coast of Scotland, northern England, the West Country and Eire.
Season: All year round; good catches made JUNE/JULY/AUGUST/SEPTEMBER.
Favourite feeding places: Deep offshore water. Big ling mostly feed near the seabed; depths of 50 fathoms (91.44 m) and below yield large catches, especially over wrecks and rocks. Ling may pursue shoals of fish to mid-water level and sometimes swim close to the surface – chasing behind and well below trawlers, ready to snatch fish falling from nets.
Successful baits: Whole fresh fish (herring, mackerel, squid, pouting) or fish strips.

Artificial baits: sizeable pirks, with baited hook.

Right methods and rigs include:
Shore fishing: Basic leger (see rig, page 114) with a wire trace (see page 120) attaching hook to swivel on line; cast into deep water.
Boat fishing: Boat leger (see rig, page 118) with a wire trace (see page 120) attaching hook to swivel on line; running paternoster (see rig, page 115) with a wire trace (see page 120) attaching hook to swivel on line; driftlining (see page 121) with a wire trace (see page 120) attaching hook to swivel on line – fish the driftline deep; jigging (see page 122) with a wire trace (see page 120) attaching pirk to line.

EXPERT TIPS
1. Use big baits to catch large ling. A whole live pouting or freshly killed mackerel is merely a snack to monster ling!
2. Stop hooked ling lunging down into rocks, caves or subterranean tunnels, or you'll lose the ling in a seabed tangle. Halt the ling's dive for freedom; fight it to the surface without surrendering line!

MACKEREL *(Scomber scombrus).*
Family: Scombridae.
Average weight: Big rod-caught mackerel can weigh 1.58 Kg (3½ lbs) or above. The average mackerel weighs about 0.56 Kg (1¼ lbs).

18. Mackerel

Description: Streamlined; glistening, metal-blue/green body; wavy black bands along the back.
*** Mackerel are good to eat (see Ch 13).

Catch mackerel! Hints:
Best locations: All round coasts of British Isles in summer.
Season: Begin arriving along the coast in MAY/JUNE; stay through JULY/AUGUST; depart about SEPTEMBER/OCTOBER. The largest catches are frequently made in AUGUST.
Favourite feeding places: On or near the surface over any type of seabed. Always on the move; chasing shoals of small fish across the ocean.
Successful baits: Live sandeels; fish strips (mackerel, herring, pilchard, sprat).

Right methods and rigs include:
Shore fishing: (pier, jetty, harbour wall, rocks): Sliding float (see rig, page 111); spinning (see trace, page 120), also spinning from a steep sloping shore.
Boat fishing: Sliding float (see rig, page 111); driftlining (see page 121); trolling (see page 122); feathering (see page 121); fly fishing, using freshwater fly fishing tackle, techniques, and specially tied flies, or large artificial trout flies.

EXPERT TIPS
1. Groundbait (see page 13) is effective.
2. Gulls wheel and dive above surface-feeding mackerel shoals; watch for their position.
3. Mackerel will pursue shoals of small fish into estuaries (see Ch 7) and occasionally well up river!

MULLET, THICK-LIPPED *(Chelon labrosus).*
Family: Mugilidae.
Average weight: Big rod-caught thick-lipped mullet can weigh 3.62 Kg (8 lbs) or above. The average thick-lipped mullet weighs about 1 Kg (2¼ lbs).

Description: Grey-blue back; silvery sides and belly. Dark grey-brown stripes along each side.
NOTE: Of similar shape, though less numerous and smaller average size are:
    THIN-LIPPED MULLET *(Liza ramada);* as the name

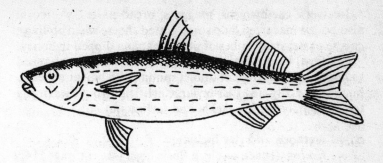

19. Thick-Lipped Mullet

suggests, thinner lips than its cousin; average weight about 0.68 Kg (1½ lbs).

GOLDEN GREY MULLET *(Liza aurata);* comparatively rare in British waters. The golden grey mullet has easily seen gold patches on its gill covers. Average weight about 340g (12 oz).

Collectively these three species are called GREY MULLET and may be caught using similar methods, rigs and baits.

Mullet are not generally considered good to eat.

Catch mullet! Hints:

Best locations: All round British Isles, Northern Ireland and Eire. Abundant in the south of England, West Country and southern Eire.

Season: Feed mainly through the summer and autumn months; MAY/JUNE/JULY/AUGUST/SEPTEMBER/OCTOBER. Mullet also feed in warm winter and spring weather; throughout the year in some "warm" harbour and estuary waters of southern England.

Favourite feeding places: At the water bottom; mid-water and frequently near or at the surface. Harbours, estuaries; many metres (even kilometres!) up tidal rivers; round rock outcrops, pier and jetty supports, bays, coves and creeks. The mullet is quite content to swim and feed in surprisingly shallow water – barely covering its back!

Successful baits: Small ragworm; little strips of fresh fish (mackerel, herring, pilchard); small crabs (soft-backed), shrimps, prawns (peeled).

In rivers: earthworms, maggots, bread paste, sweetcorn; also boiled macaroni (add some grated cheese when boiling); cheese paste; small cubes of peeled banana dipped in honey!

Artificial baits: small flounder spoons (with bait attached to hook); special angler's mullet spoon (with bait attached to hook); specially tied flies or large artificial trout flies (using freshwater fly fishing tackle and technique).

Right methods and rigs include:
Shore fishing: (beach or pier): Basic leger (see rig, page 114); simple paternoster (see rig, page 115).
Harbour wall, rocks, pier, jetty, river bank: Light float (see rig, page 111); spinning (see trace, page 120); fly fishing (freshwater style).
Dinghy fishing (harbour, estuary, close inshore): Basic leger (see rig, page 114); simple paternoster (see rig, page 115); spinning (see trace, page 120).

EXPERT TIPS
1. Freshwater fishing tackle and small freshwater fishing hooks and baits (see above) may be used to catch mullet feeding "up river".
2. The best time to catch mullet is dawn/daybreak, when the tide is rising.
3. Mullet shoals invariably follow the flood tide into rivers and withdraw on the ebb tide.
4. Be quiet, crouch low and keep out of sight; mullet are shy and sudden movement or unexpected sound send the shoal scooting for cover.
5. Mullet forage through weed for food; check heavily-weeded pier and jetty supports, hulls of moored boats and harbour walls for frequented "food larders".
6. Groundbaiting (see page 13) is effective.
7. Surface-feeding mullet in rivers can be caught by fishing your line greased 1 metre (3 ft) from the hook towards reel with freshwater fly fishing line grease; bait the hook with a small square of fresh bread crust and cast your bread upon the water. No float or weights necessary.
8. Mullet suck food into their mouth, so tighten your line the

second a bite is seen, felt or indicated by a bobbing float, or the bait may be sucked off your hook!

9. Mullet have exceptionally soft lips. Don't tighten your line too smartly or the hook tears out. Always use a long-handled landing-net or drop net (see page 95) to lift mullet from the water.

10. Shy mullet shoals are scared away by the sound of a hooked mullet splashing in the water; direct captured mullet away from the main shoal with your rod; get it out of the water as quickly and quietly as possible.

MULLET CAN BE TRICKY FISH TO CATCH!

PLAICE *(Pleuronectes platessa).*
Family: Pleuronectidae.
Average weight: Big rod-caught plaice can weigh 2.26 Kg (5 lbs) or above. The average plaice weighs about 1 Kg (2¼ lbs).

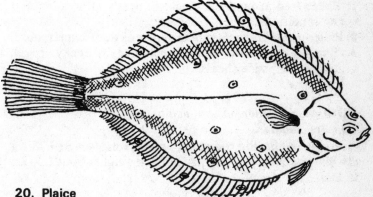

20. Plaice

Description: Brown back, dotted with large bright orange spots; white underside. Smaller head; slimmer body and smaller tail fin than the flounder, which it closely resembles. *** Plaice are good to eat (see Ch 13).

Catch plaice! Hints:
Best locations: Widespread around British Isles.

Season: Best catches are made in APRIL/MAY/JUNE/JULY/ AUGUST/SEPTEMBER/OCTOBER. Plaice stay fairly close inshore until about January, when they move into deeper offshore water to spawn; returning close to shore around April/May.

Favourite feeding places: On the bottom of sand, shell-grit/gravel, sand/mud seabed, beneath about 6 fathoms (10.97 m) of water.

Successful baits: Ragworm, lugworm, shellfish (mussels, cockles), shrimps, hermit crabs.

Right methods and rigs include:

Shore fishing: Basic leger (see rig, page 114); 2 hook running leger (see rig, page 117).

Boat fishing: Boat leger (see rig, page 118); 2 hook running leger (see rig, page 117).

EXPERT TIPS

1. Plaice feed around the clock, in nearly all weather and water conditions.

2. Plaice travel in shoals; where you hook one – expect more!

3. Patches of seabed sand surrounded by rocky, rough ground draw plaice shoals.

POLLACK *(Pollachius pollachius).*
Family: Gadidae.
Average weight: Big rod-caught pollack can weigh 7.25 Kg (16 lbs) or above. The average pollack weighs about 2.26 Kg (5 lbs).

21. Pollack

Description: Dark, olive-green back; gold/silver sides; silver-white belly. Lower jaw protrudes.
* Pollack may be cooked and eaten (see Ch 13).

Catch pollack! Hints:

Best locations: Notable specimens are caught in deep water off the West Country, and southern Eire; though pollack can be caught from many rocky areas round the British Isles.
Season: All year round; best inshore sport, MAY/JUNE/JULY/AUGUST/SEPTEMBER. Pollack withdraw into deeper offshore waters from mid-October to April.
Favourite feeding places: Close to the base of weed-covered rocks and reefs, and wrecks.
Successful baits: Whole fresh small fish (sprats, pilchards, sandeels) or fish strips (mackerel, herring); ragworms, prawns, peeler crabs, shrimps.
   Artificial baits: rubber or plastic sandeels; spoons; devon minnows; pirks.

Right methods and rigs include:

Shore fishing: (from rocks, piers, jetties, harbour walls): Sliding float (see rig, page 111); rotten bottom (see rig, page 119) cast onto rocky seabed; spinning (see trace, page 120); driftlining (see page 121).
Boat fishing: Driftlining (see page 121); trolling (see page 122); pirk "jigging" (see page 122); feathering (see page 121); rotten bottom (see rig, page 119) fished over rough or rocky seabed.

EXPERT TIPS

1. Live small fish, hooked through the upper jaw behind the lip, make successful bait.
2. Dawn and dusk often bring the best sport; when pollack rise to feed near the surface.
3. During daytime pollack usually stay deep; close to the seabed and tight against rocks.
4. Stop hooked pollack diving amongst rocks and snapping your line! Keep line taut and reel-in fast.
5. Pollack swim in shoals; once you've located a shoal, expect a fine catch of fish!
6. The biggest pollack are caught above rocks, and especially wrecks in deep offshore water.

POUTING *(Trisopterus luscus).*
Family: Gadidae.
Average weight: Big rod-caught pouting can weigh 1 Kg
(2¼ lbs) or above. The average pouting weighs about 0.56 Kg
(1¼ lbs).

22. Pouting

Description: Red-brown/copper coloured, deep body; 4 – 5
dark bands on sides. Black spot at base of pectoral fins.
Small barbule (feeler) underneath chin.
    Pouting are not generally considered good to eat.

Catch pouting! Hints:
Best locations: Common round most areas of British Isles,
particularly southern Britain and Eire.
Season: All year. Close inshore shallow water during
JUNE/JULY/AUGUST/SEPTEMBER. Withdraws to the greater
warmth of deeper water OCTOBERish to MAY.
Favourite feeding places: Near, or close to, the seabed.
Sometimes rising to feed near the mid-water level. Pouting
prefer feeding over sand-grit; rough and rocky ground;
wrecks; weed-covered boulders; pier supports etc.
Successful baits: Fish strips (mackerel, herring, squid);
ragworms, lugworms, mussels, cockles, small crabs, shrimps,
prawns, sandeels, razorfish.

Right methods and rigs include:
Shore fishing: Basic leger (see rig, page 114); 2 hook
paternoster (see rig, page 116).

Piers, jetties, harbour walls: Sliding float (see rig, page 111); simple paternoster (see rig, page 115); 2 hook paternoster (see rig, page 116); 3 hook paternoster (see rig, page 116); 2 boom paternoster (see rig, page 117).

Boat fishing: Driftlining (see page 121) deep; 3 hook paternoster (see rig, page 116); 2 boom paternoster (see rig, page 117).

EXPERT TIPS

1. Groundbaiting (see page 13) is effective from piers, jetties, harbour walls or boats.

2. When fishing with float or paternoster rig, or driftlining from a boat, present your baited hook(s) between about 355 mm (14 inches) and 1 m (3 ft) from the seabed.

3. Keep small pouting off your hook by attaching a large bit of bait.

RAY, STING *(Dasyatis pastinaca).*
Family: Dasyatidae.
Average weight: Big rod-caught sting rays can weigh 18.14 Kg (40 lbs) or above. The average sting ray weighs about 6.80 Kg (15 lbs).

23. Sting Ray

Description: Brown-grey back; grey-white underneath. The ray with a sting in its tail! The long tail is endowed with a serrated arrow-like spine – its sting! WARNING: Dodge that tail. When you see you've caught a sting ray, consider cutting your line and letting it return to the sea. The sting may pierce boots and clothing and slash a wound into which venom is injected. Temporary paralysis could follow; certainly profuse bleeding. Should you be stung, hurry to the nearest hospital, or doctor.

If you're determined to take a closer look at the ray, tread on the tail *away from the sting.* Be doubly cautious – some sting rays carry *two stings*!! Why not cut it loose?

Sting rays are not generally thought good to eat.

Location: The sting ray is active in summer and autumn, mainly along the shores of southern Britain. The sting ray is hooked offshore by boat anglers, and comes close inshore, where it's caught from beach and pier. Sting ray's favourite bait seems to be ragworm or lugworm, although it eats whole small fish or fish strips lying on or near the seabed.

Please remember the warning given regarding the sting ray's sting(s).

I suggest the sting ray ought not be a species you set out to capture.

RAY, THORNBACK *(Raja clavata).*
Family: Rajidae.
Average weight: Big rod-caught thornback rays can weigh 9.07 Kg (20 lbs) or above. The average thornback ray weighs about 4.53 Kg (10 lbs).

Description: Brown/grey back with thorn-like spines. White underneath. WARNING: The spines are sharp, and so are the teeth! Handle with care.

NOTE: The *small-eyed ray* (Raja microocellata) resembles the thornback ray in shape; without thorn-like spines. The small-eyed ray has a sand-brown back, decorated (painted) with pale, curling lines and pretty markings. The average small-eyed ray weighs about 2.26 Kg (5 lbs); is common

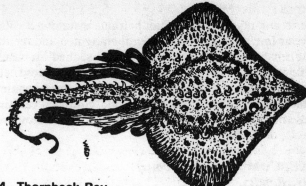

24. Thornback Ray

around the shores of southern and south-eastern Britain, and Eire. The small-eyed ray may be caught employing similar methods recommended for the thornback ray.
* Thornback rays (wings only) and small-eyed rays (wings only) may be cooked and eaten (see Ch 13).

Catch thornback rays! Hints:
Best locations: All round Britain, Northern Ireland and Eire.
Season: All year. Close inshore from MARCH/APRIL; gives excellent sport in MAY/JUNE/JULY/AUGUST/SEPTEMBER. Can be caught in deeper offshore water OCTOBER to FEBRUARY/MARCH.
Favourite feeding places: Shallow or deep water, over sand, sand/mud or clean gravel seabed; doesn't like rocks or rough ground.
Successful baits: Whole small fish (sprats) or fish strips (herring, mackerel, pilchard); sandeels; peeler, soft back and hermit crabs; shellfish; ragworms.

Right methods and rigs include:
Shore: Basic leger (see rig, page 114) with a wire trace (see page 120) of about 9.07 Kg (20 lbs) breaking strain attaching hook to swivel on line.
Boat: Boat leger (see rig, page 118) with a wire trace (see page 120) of about 9.07 Kg (20 lbs) breaking strain attaching hook to swivel on line.

EXPERT TIPS
1. Thornback rays toy with a bait before consuming it. Wait until your line pulls away strongly; then tighten and reel-in.
2. Thornback rays journey across the seabed in small, sociable groups. After one is caught and removed, the remaining thornback rays hover in the area for a fair time until moving on. During the thornbacks' "confused" waiting period, it is possible to catch the entire group, one by one!

SKATE, COMMON *(Raja batis).*
Family: Rajidae.
Average weight: Big rod-caught common skate can weigh 68 Kg (150 lbs) or above. Common skate are known to exceed 181.43 Kg (400 lbs) in weight! The average common skate weighs about 20.41 Kg (45 lbs).

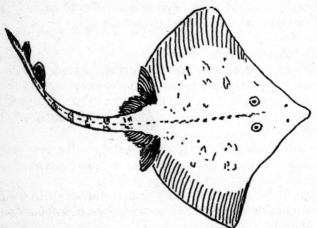

25. Common Skate

Description: Grey-brown back, "patchworked" with light-coloured blotches; blue-grey underneath.
* Common skate (wings only) may be cooked and eaten (see Ch 13).

Catch common skate! Hints:
Best locations: All round Britain; Scotland, Northern

Ireland and Eire provide the best fishing for *big* common skate.

Season: Throughout the year.

Favourite feeding places: Likes deep or shallow water over sand, sand/mud and mixed "rough" sand/rock seabed. Common skate frequently feed close inshore.

Successful baits: Wide range, especially whole fresh fish; ½ whole fish or fish strips (mackerel, herring, coalfish, pouting, pollack, whiting, squid); sandeels; crabs; shellfish; ragworms.

Right methods and rigs include:

Shore fishing: Basic leger (see rig, page 114) with a wire trace (see page 120) attaching hook to swivel on line.

Boat fishing: Boat leger (see rig, page 118) with a wire trace (see page 120) attaching hook to swivel on line.

EXPERT TIPS

1. Common skate mouth and "play" with a bait before biting; wait for a definite and strong pull on your line, then tighten and reel-in.

2. Common skate "cling" to the seabed with great power; once drawn clear, steadily pump them to the surface. Don't permit forceful downward glides back towards the bottom!

SOLE *(Solea solea).*

Family: Soleidae.

Average weight: Big rod-caught soles can weigh 1.36 Kg (3 lbs) or above. The average sole weighs about 0.56 Kg (1¼ lbs).

Description: Long, oval bodied "flatfish" (see sketch of the plaice, fig 20 on page 49). Brown/grey-green on top, with dark blotches; white underneath.

*** Soles are good to eat (see Ch 13).

Catch soles! Hints:

Best locations: Caught mainly off southern and south-eastern Britain, and southern Eire.

Season: All year; best catches usually made JUNE/JULY/AUGUST/SEPTEMBER.

Favourite feeding places: On the bottom of sand, sand/mud seabed, especially between rocks and reefs.

Successful baits: Ragworm, lugworm; small fish strips (mackerel, herring, sandeel).

Right methods and rigs include:

Shore fishing: Basic leger (see rig, page 114); 2 hook running leger (see rig, page 117).

Boat fishing: Boat leger (see rig, page 118); two hook running leger (see rig, page 117).

EXPERT TIPS

1. Soles feed mostly after dark.

2. Present your hookbait near the shore on a night-time rising tide for good catches.

TOPE *(Galeorhinus galeus).*

Family: Carcharhinidae.

Average weight: Big rod-caught tope can weigh 20.86 Kg (46 lbs) or above. The average tope weighs about 11.33 Kg (25 lbs).

26. Tope

Description: Shark! The tope is a member of the shark family. Grey/brown back, rough skin; white belly. Distinctive "notched" tail. WARNING: Beware of tope's shark-sharp teeth!

* Tope may be cooked and eaten (see Ch 13).

Catch tope! Hints:
Best locations: Widely distributed round British Isles, Northern Ireland and Eire.
Season: Feeds close inshore summer and autumn. The best months to catch tope are generally, JUNE/JULY/AUGUST/SEPTEMBER. However, big tope can be caught in deep offshore water throughout the year.
Favourite feeding places: On or near the bottom of sandy seabed, particularly near rocky ground.
Successful baits: Whole live or freshly killed fish (mackerel, dabs, herring, pouting, whiting, sprats, squid); fish strips; sandeels.

Right methods and rigs include:
Shore fishing: Basic leger (see rig, page 114) with a wire trace (see page 120) attaching hook to swivel on line; running paternoster (see rig, page 115) with a wire trace (see page 120) attaching hook to swivel on line.
Boat fishing: Boat leger (see rig, page 118) with a wire trace (see page 120) attaching hook to swivel on line; running paternoster (see rig, page 115) with a wire trace (see page 120) attaching hook to swivel on line.

EXPERT TIPS
1. Keep a tight hold on your rod; hooked tope tow unattended rods into the sea in a flash!
2. Tope feed enthusiastically on a rising tide, day or night.
3. Tope hunt alone *and* in packs. Quick unhooking; re-baiting and casting often rewards with handsome catches!

TURBOT *(Scopthalmus maximus).*
Family: Scophthalmidae.
Average weight: Big rod-caught turbot can weigh 9 Kg (20 lbs) or above. The average turbot weighs about 3.17 kg (7 lbs).

Description: Broad, speckled brown, diamond-shaped and scale-less body; covered with small and rounded bony lumps or "tubercles". White underneath.

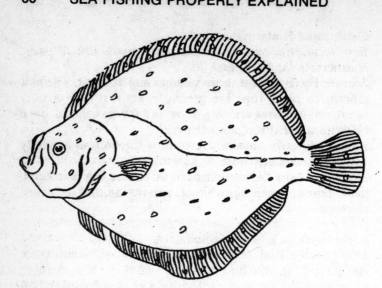

27. Turbot

*** Turbot are good to eat (see Ch 13).

Catch turbot! Hints:
Best locations: Found widely around the British Isles; caught mainly along the coast of southern and south western England; also southern Eire.
Season: Summer months give good sport, JUNE/JULY/AUGUST/SEPTEMBER. Move into deep offshore water from October to May.
Favourite feeding places: The turbot's ideal feeding station seems to be a sand or sand/mud seabed; approximately 1.2 Km (¾ mile) offshore beneath about 14 fathoms (25.6 m) of water. Sometimes seeks comfortable sandbanks in shallow water closer inshore, or descends to a convenient ambush spot in much deeper water – 40 fathoms (73.15 m) or thereabouts.
Successful baits: Small whole fish (sprats, sandeels, pouting) or strips of fresh fish (mackerel, herring).

Right methods and rigs include:
Shore fishing: Basic leger (see rig, page 114); running paternoster (see rig, page 115).
Boat fishing: Boat leger (see rig, page 118); trolling (see page 122).

EXPERT TIPS
1. Turbot like live baits best. A small fish, hooked through its upper jaw, behind the lip, is guaranteed to tempt turbot.
2. When fishing freshly-killed whole fish or fish strips; put motion into the bait by raising and lowering your rod tip at regular intervals.
3. Be gentle with hooked turbot. Hooks may rip through the soft-skinned mouth and the turbot escape! Reel-in hooked turbot with minimum applied pressure; raise the fish from the sea with a large landing net.
4. Turbot gather in small groups in good feeding places; so after you've caught number one turbot, fish a few metres further on for number two!

WEEVER, GREATER *(Trachinus draco).*

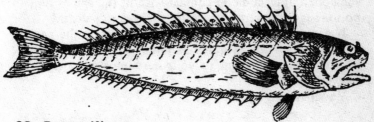

28. Greater Weever

KNOW THIS FISH: Drab yellow/brown body; sloping dark lines on sides; average weight about 227 g (½ lb). Potentially LETHAL POISON is injected by spines in the first dorsal fin and gill covers. The greater weever is an inshore AND deep-water fish – BOAT ANGLERS

BEWARE! If you hook a greater weever, carefully cut your line and let the weever drop back into the sea.

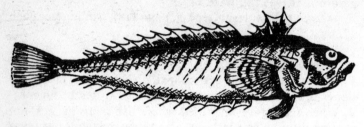

29. Lesser Weever

The tiny LESSER WEEVER *(Trachinus vipera)* – only about 152 mm (6 inches) long – is MORE VENOMOUS than its big cousin, the greater weever. Lesser weevers are inshore fish; they like to lie half buried in the seabed beneath shallow water.

WEEVERS (greater and lesser) can kill!

Sadly, people have been killed by weever venom. Happily, death is very rare and most victims of weever stings fully recover after hospital treatment. NEVER TOUCH A WEEVER and never kill a weever and leave the body where someone might come in contact with it; the spines remain poisonous for several days after the weever's death!

If a weever stings you; don't panic. Get to the nearest hospital or doctor as quick as possible. *Stay calm;* shock may cause more harm to your nervous system than the weever's venom.

You'll survive!

WHITING *(Merlangius merlangus).*
Family: Gadidae.
Average weight: Big rod-caught whiting can weigh 1.36 Kg (3 lbs) or above. The average whiting weighs about 0.45 Kg (1 lb).

Description: Large and pointed head; slim body; gold-green back and silver-white sides. Small, sharp teeth. WARNING:

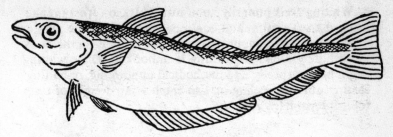

30. Whiting

Nips from whiting teeth can infect your fingers – handle with care!
*** Whiting are good to eat (see Ch 13).

Catch whiting! Hints:
Best locations: Round most parts of British Isles.
Season: Arrive inshore early autumn, SEPTEMBER/OCTOBER; stay close to shore through winter months: NOVEMBER/DECEMBER/JANUARY/FEBRUARY. Move to deeper offshore water about MARCH/APRIL.
Favourite feeding places: On or near bottom of sand, sand/mud or shell-grit seabed; will feed over rough, rocky ground and at mid-water level.
Successful baits: Ragworm, lugworm, shellfish, shrimps, prawns, sandeels, strips of fresh fish (herring, mackerel, sprat, pilchard, whiting), hermit crab.
   Artificial baits: small pirks (see fig 39 page 82) baited or unbaited and jigged (see page 122).

Right methods and rigs include:
Shore fishing: 2 hook paternoster (see rig, page 116); 3 hook paternoster (see rig, page 116).
Boat fishing: 2 hook paternoster (see rig, page 116); 2 boom paternoster (see rig, page 117); 3 hook paternoster (see rig, page 116); 2 hook running leger (see rig, page 117); driftlining (see page 121) deep.

EXPERT TIPS
1. Groundbaiting (see page 13) is effective.

2. Whiting feed hungrily soon after dusk on frosty nights when the sea's calm, and continue feeding into the night.

3. Have your bait supply ready to slip straight on the hook immediately a caught whiting is unhooked. Once whiting begin biting, speedy and methodical unhooking; re-baiting; casting out and reeling-in, can catch a fair weight of tasty food for your freezer!

WRASSE, BALLAN *(Labrus bergylta).*
WRASSE, CUCKOO *(Labrus mixtus).*
Family: Labridae.
Average weight: Big rod-caught ballan wrasse can weigh 2.72 Kg (6 lbs) or above. The average ballan wrasse weighs about 1 Kg (2¼ lbs).

Big rod-caught cuckoo wrasse can weigh 0.56 Kg (1¼ lbs) or above. The average cuckoo wrasse weighs about 227 g (½ lb).

31. Cuckoo Wrasse

Description: Male cuckoo wrasse: brilliant blue back; orange-gold sides. Female cuckoo wrasse: vivid pink-red body; black spots on back.

Ballan wrasse: green or red/rust-brown body; sometimes infused with blue. Pale orange/white underneath. Colour pattern variable. Breeding ballan wrasse build nests to lay their eggs in!

Wrasse are not generally considered good to eat.

Catch wrasse! Hints:
Best locations: The BALLAN WRASSE is found round most of the British coast. The CUCKOO WRASSE is caught mainly along the shores of southern Britain.
Season: Wrasse are especially active close inshore during MAY/JUNE/JULY/AUGUST/SEPTEMBER/OCTOBER.
Favourite feeding places: Near the base of inshore rocks; slightly offshore rocks; weed-covered reefs; old holed and cracked harbour walls; sandy patches of seabed between rocks and/or reefs. Where there are rocks you'll likely find wrasse!
Successful baits: Sandeels, small pieces of fresh fish (herring, mackerel, pilchard, squid); ragworms, lugworms; small shellfish (cockles, mussels, limpets); prawns, peeler crabs, soft-backed crabs.

Right methods and rigs include:
Shore fishing: Rotten bottom (see rig, page 119) cast onto sandy area near rocks.
Rocks and harbour walls: Sliding float (see rig, page 111); rotten bottom (see rig, page 119).

EXPERT TIPS
1. A rising tide frequently brings large catches of wrasse.
2. Wrasse hustle together very close to the rock face, so position your baited hook near as you're able to the rocks.
3. Don't let wrasse tangle your line round rocks. Reel-in hooked wrasse fast!
4. You'll need a long-handled landing net or drop net (see page 95) to hoist hooked wrasse to a convenient unhooking place.
5. Float fished baits are often most effective presented about 304 mm (1 ft) above the point where rock base meets seabed – the bottom. However, if your bait doesn't soon attract bites, adjust the float to raise the bait a bit further from the bottom, 304 mm (1 ft) at a time; until you find the popular feeding level of the moment, and begin catching wrasse!

4

QUALITY TACKLE FOR THAT PERFECT EDGE

Even expert skill won't overcome disaster if you hook a powerful fish on cheap, inferior tackle. For superior results buy the best tackle you can afford. Good tackle gives you a winning edge over big and strong, fighting fish. Buy best and always be the winner!

Correctly balanced tackle is essential to achieve ultimate angling performance. The only certain way to buy the right tackle for the type of sea fishing you want to enjoy, is to visit your local specialist tackle dealer's shop and ask his professional advice.

Be wise, buy right and have no cause for regret. Quality tackle lends you that perfect edge!

Rods (see also the "suitable rods" sections in Chapters 7 to 11).
Suitable rods for different types of sea angling are suggested in the "Tackle Notes" sections of Chapters 7 to 11.

Beach casting rods (see also page 93): specially designed to cast heavy weights far into the surf of breaking waves where fish feed. Beach rods are built to cast a specified range of weights from 85 g (3 oz) to 255 g (9 oz). Details are supplied with new rods. NEVER EXCEED the maximum weight recommended for your rod, or it might break!

Boat rods (see also page 104): sold according to "line class". A 9.07 Kg (20 lbs) line class boat rod is made to fish most effectively with line of 9.07 Kg (20 lbs) breaking strain.

You may fish with line 2.26 Kg (5 lbs) either side of the stated "line class" *but no more,* or you won't get the best "balanced" action from rod and line.

Reels
Suitable reels for different types of sea angling are suggested in the "Tackle Notes" sections of Chapters 7 to 11.

Fixed spool reels: easy to operate and perfect for the beginner fishing on shore. The reel's spool is "fixed" and unmoving; line simply strips off the spool when cast.

Multiplier reels cast line from a rotating drum; ideal for boat fishing, and reeling-in very heavy fish when shore angling (especially from tall rocks, piers and high harbour walls). A degree of skill is required to beach cast successfully with a multiplier, though once mastered, championship-class casts are possible with multiplier reels.

Ask your specialist tackle dealer to help you match rod and reel. A harmonious balance of weight and design brings amazing results.

Line (see also "Tackle Notes" sections of Chapters 7 to 11). Never buy "cut-price" line. Cheap line can't cope with big catches – it snaps! Fill fixed spool reels neatly to the spool lip with line. Fill multiplier reels with line evenly to the drum rim.

Weights
Also called "sinkers"; come in many shapes and sizes (see "Tackle Notes" sections of Chapters 7 to 11). "Balls", "bombs", "pears" and "torpedoes" are the best shapes for general use.

Weights fitted with grapnel wires grip the seabed in rough conditions, slowing tidal shift of the baited hook. Use the smallest weight necessary to hold your bait at the depth and position you expect fish to be feeding.

Hooks
High quality, non-brittle hooks sharpen to a proper chisel-edge. Check that the points are fish-hooking sharp before angling. Use an angler's sharpening stone to hone hook points to perfection.

Hook sizes
Sea hook sizes graduate from "small" sizes 6 or 4; 2 or 1 and

1/0 to giant size 10/0 or 12/0.

Match hook size to bait size and fish size. Use generous helpings of bait on large hooks to catch "specimen" size big fish.

Small hook sizes 6 or 4 are adequate for smaller fish: dabs, flounders, garfish, mackerel, wrasse etc.

Small hook sizes 2 or 1 are suitable for "smallish" fish: bass, young cod ("codling"), dabs, flounders, mullet, whiting etc.

Medium hook sizes 1/0 or 2/0 or 3/0 are suitable for larger fish: bass, cod, dogfish, skates, rays, whiting etc.

Big hook sizes 4/0 or 6/0 are suitable for bigger fish: cod, conger eels, dogfish, rays, skates, tope etc.

Monster hook sizes 8/0 and 10/0 or 12/0 are suitable for huge fish: tope, halibut, skates, sharks, Kraken and Leviathan (see page 8) etc.

Beginners usually find hook sizes 2 or 1 or 1/0 satisfactory for general sea fishing. Increase bait size and hook size where BIG fish are expected.

Extras

Invaluable items of tackle stocked by your specialist dealer and freely available for inspection in his shop include:

Tackle boxes and anglers' *haversacks, rucksacks* or *daypacs.*

Tackle boxes are neat and provide a seat but if you have to walk a distance, a rucksack may be better as it sits snug on your back.

Don't forget *boots* and *clothing*; sea anglers' *hook disgorgers* and *artery forceps* for removing hooks from fishes' mouths; *long-nosed pliers* to cut wire and line; *reel lubricant* and *small spanners* for re-fastening bits of rod and reel before they drop off!

Your local tackle shop is an Aladdin's cave of angling treasures. Browse round and be a regular customer. Support your local specialist tackle dealer and he'll be delighted to help you with advice, hints and tips. You can't manage without him!

TACKLE HINT

Salt water corrodes almost anything from leather boots to rod rings and reels. Rinse tackle taken sea fishing with cold tap water before drying, cleaning and storing.

SUPERHOOKERS

12 TOP TACKLE TIPS To Improve Your Fishing Pleasure

1. Hoard plastic bags of all sizes. Take a few on each fishing trip to keep spare clothing and tackle dry. Large, heavy-gauge plastic bin liners are useful for caught fish destined for the freezer. Special heavy-duty, self sealing plastic bags (available in several sizes) are sold by tackle dealers.

2. Make sure any fishing jacket or waterproofs worn aren't too tight across your shoulders, or under the arms. Tight clothes cramp casting style.

3. Stripes of bright paint or fluorescent strips on tackle box, bag or rucksack, show their position clearly should light conditions fade after you've wandered from them.

4. A roll of waterproof electrical insulating tape is ideal for temporary patching of splits and tears in tackle or clothing; frayed rod whippings, and loose rod or reel fittings.

5. To prevent sand damaging the working parts of reels, rod rings and joints (ferrules) keep reels in reel cases until ready for use; assemble rods before reaching the beach. Brush sand and grit from tackle with a small, soft paintbrush before packing for your homeward journey.

6. An angler's umbrella gives welcome protection from strong winds on exposed beaches. Anchor the umbrella with umbrella guy ropes fitted to the top; tied to tent pegs fixed in the ground and covered with heavy stones.

7. A drop of rod varnish or waterproof Superglue on a well tied knot in fishing line increases the knot's strength.

8. Never put used wet hooks with unused dry hooks. Smear used hooks with angler's pilchard oil to counter the corrosive action of salt water; keep them separate from unused hooks until you've dried and sharpened them.

9. Hooked small ragworm or lugworm baits; soft baits like mussels, and "cocktails" of mixed small and/or soft baits that seem unlikely to stay on the hook after a long, hook jarring cast, are easily stuck to one another and/or the hook with a tiny dollop of waterproof Superglue – which scrapes off hooks with a sharp knife. Don't glue your fingers to the hookbait!

10. An angler's battery-operated headlamp is a boon when fishing after dusk; fastened to your forehead by its comfortable headband, the headlamp leaves your hands free and beams light wherever you look (be safe; have a torch handy for extra instant light).

11. Strips of angler's luminous sticky tape wrapped around your rod at joints and tip show what's happening to the rod when fishing after dark. A fluorescent rod tip is valuable as an after-dusk bite indicator (see page 14).

12. When shore fishing in cold winter weather, or icy after dark hours, pack a camper's plastic "bivvy" or "survival" bag. If you fancy a break, pull the bag up over your legs and chest and enjoy a warming and revitalizing sit down snack.

5

BEST BAITS FOR BITES

Any small creature which lives where fish feed can be put on a hook, cast into the water, and catch fish! If in doubt – try it out! Some baits attract fishes better than others.

The best baits for bites vary from one species of fish to another (see Ch 3) and from one area to another. Pop into the local specialist tackle shop for accurate advice and a supply of fresh, fish-catching bait.

Before collecting bait from the shore, check by-laws (if not displayed on a noticeboard near the shore, visit or 'phone the public reference library) to be certain bait-gathering and digging is permitted. Take a plastic bucket and lid; one or two sea angler's large plastic bait boxes and a few old newspapers. A full-size garden fork is necessary for digging. Remember to rinse the fork under tap water at home afterwards; oil metal parts to prevent rusting.

SAFETY HINTS
* Tread warily when collecting baits at low tide; be alert for soft "sinking" mud and quicksand!
* Fill in and smooth over holes and hollows dug; *before* someone stumbles into them!
* Watch for Weevers (see page 61) lying under shallow water.

TIPS
1. Buy or gather bait the day you go fishing to be sure of fish-attracting freshness.
2. Keep fresh bait covered, in a cool place out of sunshine.
3. Never mix in the same container, baits likely to EAT each other. For instance, ragworms eat lugworms!
4. Use damaged freshly gathered baits immediately, they won't live long!
5. Stored bait: discard unhealthy looking, injured or dead specimens.

6. Baits can be hooked singly; in bunches; or in "cocktail" assortments. Ragworm or lugworm and shellfish (mussels, cockles, limpets etc.) is a favourite "cocktail" with many greedy fishes.

7. Big fish prefer big baits; small fish seize small baits. Choose your bait size and hook size (see page 67) according to the species of fish you're hunting.

8. Improve appeal of drab looking baits with a squeeze of angler's pilchard oil.

9. Use a *sharp* filleting knife and securely placed cutting board when slicing fish for bait, and aim to *miss* your fingers!

32. Mussels and cockles
 Above: Mussels on rock
 Below: Cockles fresh dug from sand

Best Baits

CLAMS (shellfish): Live burrowed in sand and sand/mud, about 304 mm (1 ft) beneath the surface. Prise open shell with a strong thin-bladed knife, and remove soft clam; thread on hook so the clam's tough "foot" is held firm on the hook's bend below the barbed hookpoint.

COCKLES (shellfish): Live burrowed in sand, sand/mud, or mud/ about 25 mm (1 inch) beneath the surface. Prise open the shell with a strong thin-bladed knife and remove cockle; thread hook through cockle so the flesh is held firm on the hook's bend below the barbed hookpoint.

CRABS, COMMON: Shore or "green" crabs are called *peeler* crabs when they are about to "peel" or shed an outgrown shell ready to harden their skin into a new, bigger shell. As soon as a "peeler" crab has peeled the old shell, it's known as a *soft-backed* crab. After several days, the new shell has hardened and the crab is termed a *hard-backed* crab.

Peeler and soft backed crabs make excellent bait for many species of fish. They can usually be found from May/June onwards, throughout the summer, at low tide in rock pools, shallow bays, estuaries and harbours. Crabs have favourite places to peel; once located, you can return for a regular supply.

Search for "peelers" and "soft backs" under stones, weed, breakwaters, pier or jetty supports etc. Mating female "peelers", may be found clinging for safety to the underside of hard-backed males, who will fight to defend them!

A peeler crab is identifiable by its old, soon-to-be-peeled shell – which looks dull and brittle. It comes away easily if tapped with a knife handle or stone. A soft-backed crab is betrayed by its new-looking, soft-skinned back.

Crabs, not wanted for immediate use, may be kept alive for a few days in a large loosely-covered (not airtight!) plastic bucket containing damp sand and seaweed; stored in a cool, shaded place. Don't mix peelers and soft backs, and if they become hard-backed, take them to the shore and release them. Hard-backed crabs seldom make successful bait.

Kill crabs by stabbing between the eyes with a sharp knife. Remove claws; insert your hook through the crab's belly from its side. Push the hookpoint out of the crab's back, so the crab rests on the hook's bend below the barbed hookpoint. To be sure your hook isn't torn from the crab by casting, rough water or cunning fish: bunch together and bind the crab's side legs to your hook's long shank with a few turns of strong elastic thread, knotted tightly.

An alternative way of fastening a freshly killed crab to your hook using strong elastic thread, is shown in fig 36 on page 78. Break off the claws; strip away the shell and use the claw flesh as separate bait.

A large crab can be killed and sliced in half lengthways, to provide 2 generous-size baits. A crab may also be broken into pieces, and the shelled flesh threaded on small hooks to catch fish.

CRABS, HERMIT (shellfish): Live in "borrowed" empty shells – graduating from small periwinkle shells to large whelk shells as the hermit crab grows in size. Small hermit crabs can be found in rock pools at low tide. Large hermit crabs live in deeper offshore water, and are often sold to sea anglers by commercial fishermen. Crack open the shell to remove the crab for hooking. Use either the tail only, or the whole freshly-killed crab, threaded onto the hook through its soft underneath (see fig 36 on page 78). Break off legs and claws to bleed scent into the water and make the crab obviously vulnerable and appealing to inquisitive fish.

EARTHWORMS (lobworms): Gather from soil and damp grass. Earthworms are an effectve bait for estuary- and river-feeding sea fish (see Ch 7). Earthworms don't live long in saltwater and aren't suitable for saltwater sea fishing. Thread on hook singly or in small bunches (see fig 35 on page 77).

FISH: Catch your own fish for bait, or buy freshly-caught fish from a coastal fishmonger, or purchase direct from local commercial fishermen at the quayside.

Fresh herrings, mackerel, sprats and pilchards make the best all-round fish baits, because their natural oil content is high.

TIP
OIL:BLOOD:GUTS = SCENT

SCENT = BIG FISH INVESTIGATING!

Deep-frozen herrings and squid (your own or shop-bought) and sandeels also prove good bait; some species of fish become too soft to stay long on the hook after being deep-frozen.

Squid is a handy all-round bait; every part of a squid may be cut up and used to catch fish. Squid can also be fished whole (see fig 36 on page 78) to attract *big* fish.

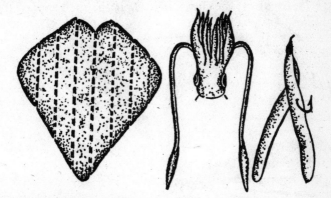

33. Using squid as bait
 Left: Body and flap cut into strips
 Middle: Head
 Right: Strips of squid on hook; tied at top with thread to prevent slipping

Any fresh fish offered as bait could appeal to predators. Consistently successful fish baits include: coalfish, small cod, garfish, pollack, pouting, whiting.

Hook live fish through the upper jaw, behind the lip; freshly killed whole or halved fish may be hooked through eye sockets; or your line pulled through the length of a whole freshly killed fish (see fig 36 on page 78) using an angler's baiting needle. Bind the tail end of the fish bait with thread or elastic, to stop line cutting free from the flesh.

Slice bait fish into chunks, fillets or strips of suitable size to excite the fish you're pursuing. Mackerel "lasks" (see fig 34 over) cut from fresh mackerel, almost always guarantee big bass catches when trolled (see page 122) in summertime.

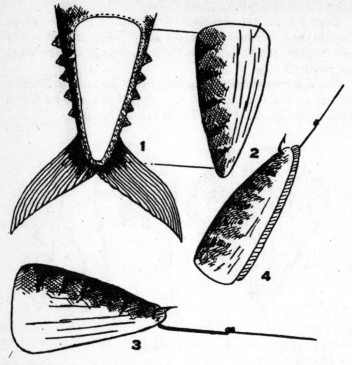

34. Making a lask

TIP
Strips of fish, cut in shapes to resemble small fish, especially a tapered sandeel shape, are extraordinarily successful bait!

LIMPETS, COMMON (shellfish): Collected from rocks at low tide, common limpets attract some rock-feeding fish (wrasse, black bream etc.), but are mainly added to bait "cocktails" (see page 72) and crushed for groundbait (see page 13). When used as hookbait, carefully scoop limpet out of shell with a strong thin-bladed knife and thread on hook so the tough "foot" is held firm on the hook's bend below the barbed hookpoint.

LIMPETS, SLIPPER (shellfish): Live clustered together in shallow-water colonies; males on top, females underneath

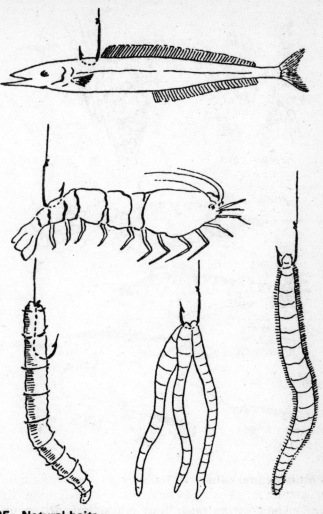

35. Natural baits
Top: Sandeel
Middle: Prawn
Below: Lugworm, earthworms, ragworm

(see fig 37, page 79). Heavy seas wash slipper limpets ashore in large numbers. Prise shell clusters apart with a strong thin-bladed knife, carefully scoop out slipper limpet and

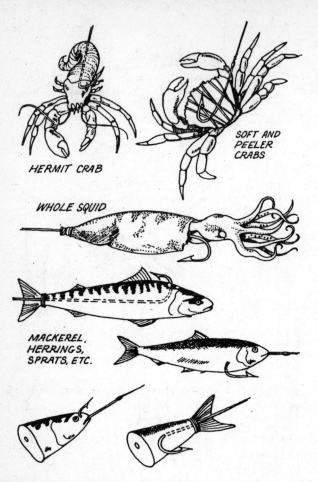

HERMIT CRAB

SOFT AND
PEELER
CRABS

WHOLE SQUID

MACKEREL,
HERRINGS,
SPRATS, ETC.

36. More natural baits

thread on hook so the tough "foot" is held firm on the hook's bend below the barbed hookpoint.

LUGWORMS: Live burrowed about 0.45 m (1½ ft) beneath sand or sand/mud in U-shaped tunnels, topped by coiled "casts" of ejected lugworm excrement. Lugworms average about 152 mm (6 inches) in length, and may be dug at low tide. Store lugworms not wanted immediately as bait, spaced

37. Limpet baits
Above: Common limpet adhering to piece of flint
Below: Little colony of slipper limpets growing together on
a piece of rock

roughly 76 mm (3 inches) apart from each other on sheets of
clean dry newspaper, folded into a large plastic bait box, or
large plastic bag pricked with a few air holes, and placed
somewhere cool. Lugworms are best used fresh, but can be
stored in a fridge for 3 days. They *stink* when dead and
decomposing!

Thread onto hook through the lugworm's head, or at the
point where the lugworm's thin tail meets the thicker trunk
of its body. Some sea anglers tear off the tail before casting –
to release fish-luring juices.

MUSSELS (shellfish): Gather at low tide from pier and jetty
supports, harbour walls, breakwaters, and exposed rocks.
Prise open shell with a strong thin-bladed knife and carefully
remove mussel OR take mussels home and keep for 1 to 3
days in a covered plastic bucket containing damp sand and
seaweed; stored somewhere cool. Shortly before setting out

fishing, drop mussels into warm, slightly salted water; remove mussels from their shells as soon as the shells open. Place a few drops of angler's pilchard oil on mussels to restore scent evaporated by warm water and wrap in plastic bag. Thread mussel on hook so the tough "foot" is held firm on the hook's bend below the barbed hookpoint.

PRAWNS: Can be netted throughout summer months in rock pools at low tide; use a long-handled child's beach net. Prawns are most effective as bait fished alive. Dead or alive, thread on hook through the second or third segment of the tail (see fig 35 on page 77).

RAGWORMS: Live burrowed in sand, sand/mud and mud. There are many kind of ragworm; ranging in length from 25 mm (1 inch) to "King" ragworm growing as long as 0.91 m (3 ft)! Ragworms vary in colour from white or green, to the more familiar brown or bright red. The common ragworm is about 114 mm (4½ inches) in length and brown-bronze coloured.

A ragworm's head houses extendable sharp jaws; large ragworms can give your fingers a painful nip!

Ragworms may be dug at low tide from estuaries, beaches, and harbours. Keep ragworms not wanted for immediate use wrapped between layers of clean, dry newspaper – leave a space of approximately 76 mm (3 inches) between individual ragworms; fold the newspaper and carefully place in a large plastic bait box, or large plastic bag with a few pricked air holes. Ragworms, though best used fresh, may be stored in a fridge for about 6 days.

Thread onto hook below the ragworm's head (see fig 35 on page 77), or push the hook into its mouth and slide ragworm along the whole length of the hook's shank; bring the hookpoint out through the ragworm's side. Very long ragworms may be broken in half or into several pieces before placing on one hook, or used to bait several hooks.

RAZORFISH (shellfish): Live burrowed in sand, sand/mud, or mud; just below the surface, near the low tide line. Prise open the shell with a strong thin-bladed knife and remove the razorfish; thread on hook so the razorfish's tough "foot" is held firm on the hook's bend below the barbed hookpoint.

SANDEELS: Live on sandy seabeds, in estuaries; close inshore and offshore to a depth of about 20 fathoms (36.57 m). Sandeels often disappear from shallow inshore waters in autumn, returning about May. Sandeels burrow beneath sand to a depth of about 203 mm (8 inches). They can be uncovered by raking wet sand at low tide, in "zig-zag" patterns (see fig 38 below).

Insert hook through body behind the sandeel's head (see fig 35 on page 77), or through the sandeel's mouth, so the hook's bend and barbed point project from its throat or belly. A sandeel with head cut off; hooked onto an angler's dead bait mount (available from tackle dealers) and clipped to the link swivel on a spinning trace (see page 120) is a deadly attractive natural spinning bait!

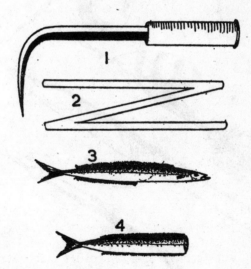

38. Sandeels
1. Rake-hook for getting sandeels out of the sand.
2. Zig-zag method of raking the sand
3. Sandeel
4. Sandeel with head and shoulders cut off; an excellent natural bait for spinning

PRESERVED BAITS
Several popular natural baits, specially treated and preserved, are sold by tackle shops as "preserved baits". These baits are second-best to fresh natural baits, but convenient and sometimes reasonably effective. A liberal squeeze of angler's pilchard oil applied before fishing, restores much of the bait's appetizing appeal. Among successful preserved baits are: lugworm, ragworm, shrimp, sprat, and chopped squid.

39. Artificial baits
   1. Mackerel spinner; *2.* Flounder spoon; *3.* Bass and mullet spinner; *4.* Sandeel lure; *5.* Pirk.

ARTIFICIALS

Spinners and *spoons*, many of which can be baited with a tasty morsel of fishes' favourite fresh foods, are designed for spinning (see trace, page 120); *pirks* for "jigging" (see page 122) and *sandeel* lures for spinning (see page 120) or trolling (see page 122).

Artificials rely on movement, vibration, shape and colour to lure and excite fish into seizing them. Many highly successful artificial baits are on sale to today's sea angler.

6

BETTER SAFE THAN DEAD

The sea is not our friend. The sea is neutral; it could offer us a big fish and drown us – with the same wave! Every year sea anglers drown, sadly the number is increasing. Where relevant, Chapters in this book give clear safety hints; take note of them and survive!

And study Chapter 3, "Get Fish Wise" for details of dangerous fish with skin-tearing teeth, and slashing spines or stings. Given half-a-chance, some fish would eat anglers for breakfast – snap, crackle and pop!

CLOTHING
Dress to stay warm, dry and smiling. Wear a woolly hat; carry a full set of waterproofs and spare pullover.

Put on some bright coloured clothing to give rescuers clear sight of you in the event of accident.

SNACKS
Don't forget to take a packed lunch, flask of hot soup and a couple of chocolate bars for emergencies. Leave the brandy-filled hip flask at home. Brandy doesn't warm you, quite the reverse – alcohol lowers your body temperature.

GENERAL SAFETY HINTS
* Tell someone where you intend fishing, and when to expect you back.
* Go fishing with a friend.
* Always carry an EMERGENCY SURVIVAL KIT which ought to include: *waterproof torch* + *spare bulb* and *batteries*.

The S.O.S. signal is ...._____... ; dot (short flash), dot, dot; dash (longer flash), dash, dash; dot, dot, dot. Repeat until answered.

The S.O.S. signal may also be made by reflecting sunlight from a mirror or polished metal.

Take a *whistle* as part of your kit. The international distress signal with a whistle is 6 short blasts in one minute; wait one minute, then repeat.

Map and *compass* (know how to use them). Sudden thick fog blots out familiar landmarks.

First aid kit: assorted plasters, roll of bandage, safety pins, antiseptic cream and pain killing tablets.

FOUR GOLDEN TIPS

1. Under qualified supervision, learn to swim *at least* 50 m (55 yd) fully clothed.

2. Learn basic first aid at evening classes run by the Red Cross, St. John Ambulance Brigade; a similar organisation or qualified instructor.

3. If you find yourself in the water, stay calm and get out *quick*!!! Cold water *kills fast*.

4. Should you see someone in distress and can't immediately help, dial 999 from the nearest telephone. Ask for the police and/or coastguard; describe the exact location of the person requiring assistance.

7

ESTUARY AND HARBOUR SUCCESS SECRETS

River mouth estuaries and harbour walls are easy to fish and careful, cunning anglers bag big catches of sizeable fishes.

Estuaries
An estuary is the meeting point between outflowing fresh water and incoming tidal sea water. The resultant mixture of fresh and salt water is termed "brackish" water.

Brackish estuary water supplies rich feeding for bass, conger eels, mackerel, mullet, flounders and freshwater eels. Bass cheerfully follow the rising tide 2 or 3 kilometres up river. Mullet sometimes venture 4.82 Km (3 miles) or more inland.

Most estuary-feeding fish move into the river mouth and cruise up river on a rising tide; have a party gobbling small crabs, fish fry, lugworms, prawns, ragworms, sandeels and shrimps and freshwater fishes' usual foodstuff; then move back down river into the sea on the ebb tide.

Some fish stay in channels and pools. Flounders laze, partly buried, in water-covered sand/mud patches, waiting patiently for the next incoming tide. Small "school" bass and mullet withdraw to the security of deeper estuary water.

Fish remaining in estuary water at low tide respond to a well presented bait.

TIPS
1. As the tide begins to rise, large bass gather on the seaward side of shingle banks, sand/mud flats and sandbars, until the tidal current is high and strong enough to sweep them into the main centre channel of the river. Fishing for bass on the

seaward side of an estuary entrance in a rising tide produces
pleasing results.

2. Be ready for the run of fish passing up river on the high
tide. Stealthily follow shoals along the river bank. Be
prepared for the same shoals returning down river as the tide
ebbs.

3. Pay special attention to drainage and sewage pipe outlets –
always fruitful spots to fish; areas of sand and sand/mud
housing lugworm and ragworm; weed-covered rocks, jetties
and submerged stone steps beside moorings etc.

4. Groundbait suspended in a fine mesh bag (see page 13) or
scattered loose attracts fish.

5. Stay out of sight; be quiet, tread lightly. Kneel low to cast
bait and make no sharp, sudden movements against the sky-
line – or the fish will know you're hunting them!

Harbours

Harbours and cracks and clefts in harbour walls provide fish
with a dependable and plentiful supply of natural food;
scraps of people's discarded snacks; gutted fish offal thrown
overboard by commercial fishermen. They also insulate fish
from strong currents and wild weather conditions.

Many harbours are a haven for bass, conger eels,
flounders, mackerel, mullet, small pollack, pouting, whiting
etc.

TIPS

1. Watch for fishable eddies and deep water runs; gaps
between weeds, and beds of sand or sand/mud.

2. Conger eels often live inside holes and cracks in stone
harbour walls; outlet pipes and under sunken, rusting parts
of wrecks.

3. Groundbait suspended in a fine mesh bag (see page 13) or
scattered loose attracts fish.

4. Fish beside steps leading down to the water for easy
landing of hooked fish.

Safety Hints

* Beware of standing on estuary mud or sandbanks at low

tide. You may be swallowed!
* Stay back from the edge of harbour walls and be careful descending slippery stone steps.

Right methods and rigs for estuary and harbour wall fishing include:
Light float (see rig, page 111); sliding float (see rig, page 111); basic leger (see rig, page 114) where crabs are unlikely to seize hookbait; simple paternoster (see rig, page 115); running paternoster (see rig, page 115); 2 hook paternoster (see rig, page 116); spinning (see trace, page 120); driftlining (see page 121) and fly fishing using freshwater fly fishing tackle, techniques and artificial flies, to catch surface-feeding bass, mackerel or mullet.

Tackle Notes (see also Ch 4)
Suitable rods: sea or strong freshwater rods, from 2.74 m (9 ft) to 3.65 m (12 ft) in length.
Suitable reels: fixed spool or multiplier.
Suitable line strength: from about 3.62 Kg (8 lbs) to 5.44 Kg (12 lbs) breaking strain.
Suitable weights: up to about 56 g (2 oz) depending on the distance you wish to cast and strength of current.
    * You'll find a long-handled landing net useful; a drop net (see page 95) from high harbour walls.

8
CHAMPION BEACH CASTING

Shorefishing the tumbling surf from a beautiful beach is a refreshing and lively sport. Beach casting is a branch of sea fishing pursued and enjoyed by many champion sea anglers.

Sometimes fish, notably bass, dabs and flounders, search the seabed for food within 3.65 m (12 ft) of the shore. At other times you'll have to cast 91.5 m (100 yds) or more to put your baited hook among feeding shoals; though a cast of about 32 m (35 yds) normally finds marauding fish.

Beach casting
To learn the secrets of beach casting champions, who cast a weighted line over 228.5 m (250 yds) in casting tournaments, watch experts in action. View beach fishing and casting competitions; chat to competitors. Venues are advertised in the local and angling press. Take a course of instruction at Local Education Authority evening classes; a private course, or one run at your nearest Sports' Centre. Better still – join a sea angling club!

Basics of beach casting

40. Beach casting style

Stand comfortably with your feet apart; left foot pointing in the direction you wish to cast. Lower the rod behind you and point the tip down low towards the beach; lay 1.21 m (4 ft) to 1.82 m (6 ft) of line, including assembled and attached rig (see Ch 12), on the beach. Grip the lower end of the rod butt with your left hand; with your right hand grip the reel seating (where the reel is fastened to the rod handle). Keep your right thumb on the reel line to prevent line slipping off the fixed spool's "spool" or multiplier's "drum".

Look towards your rod tip, your left shoulder and elbow facing in the direction you're about to cast.

Begin turning your body around; look into the sky above your target area (don't stare into the sun!); bring the rod upwards as you turn.

Firmly and smoothly power the rod forwards; finally whipping the rod out straight in the direction of your target area – release the line from your reel as the weight speeds past the rod tip. Don't move your position until the weight splashes into the sea, then stop your reel.

You'll soon develop a personal style of casting that suits you best. Beach casting is an easy, co-ordinated technique, requiring little physical strength. There should be no strained muscles!

To become a champion beach caster you must have confidence and practise regularly.

Start with modest expectations – 13.5 m (15 yds). When you comfortably cast a specific distance, aim for a 9 m (10 yds) improvement. It's surprising how quickly a laboured style of casting that barely reaches 23 m (25 yds) may be nurtured into a technique effortlessly achieving 110 m (120 yds) and beyond!

How to "read" the beach.
Pick a place to fish away from car parks; holidaymakers' splashing and screeching "beach" radios. Fish stay further out to sea opposite noisy shores; often swimming along to quiet areas of beach, where they feel safe to venture closer inshore.

Spot likely patches of water from the cliff top. A telescope or binoculars help!

Study the sea for dark blotches showing the position of underwater rocks and reefs; brown spreads of seabed sand; dark blue pools of water over deep gullies and channels; light blue expanses of "shallow" water over sand, sand/mud or shingle.

Note the location of large beds of sand between rocks and rough ground, favoured by dabs, flounders, plaice and rays. Sandy and sand/mud beaches may also attract (according to locality and season, see Ch 3): bass, cod, dogfish (smoothhounds, lesser spotted dogfish, spurdog), mackerel, mullet, sole, tope, turbot and whiting.

Rocky and rough seabed draws (depending on location and season, see Ch 3): bass, bream, coalfish, cod, conger eels, dogfish (bull huss), mackerel, pollack, pouting, skates, whiting and wrasse.

Jot useful notes and/or markings on Ordnance Survey maps of the area for future references. Keep an exercise book for detailed records of observations.

Having spied the sea from above, next explore the beach itself at low tide. Look for exposed weed-covered rocks, rock pools, hollows and channels hiding small marine creatures and tiny fish; patches of sand or sand/mud.

Check for the natural foods fish will expect to find as they forage through these food-rich dining spots on the incoming tide. Depending upon the type of beach (see Ch 5), search for clams, cockles, fish fry, limpets, lugworms, mussels, prawns, ragworms, razorfish, sandeels, and shrimps. If, on the rising tide, you present a hookbait at the place fish suspect the "bait" lives naturally, you should catch fish!

Expect excellent catches on the sheltered side of breakwaters; around rocks; whirling currents and eddies; near the point where narrow streams, rivulets or drains flow into the sea; close to dense growths of weed, and power station warm water outflow pipes!

TIPS
1. Don't cast further than necessary. Heavy swells of rolling surf breaking on the shore stir up food particles and small

creatures normally buried safe from attack. A cast beyond the 3rd or 4th breaking wave ("breaker") could catch a large bass.

2. For up to 4 or 5 days after a storm, fish feed close inshore.

3. If you're not hooking fish, try further out (or closer in!) until you find where the fish are feeding.

4. Fish seldom feed over barren shingle. Cast to the edge where shingle meets sand or sand/mud.

5. On calm, clear and sunny days fish usually prefer to stay offshore until dusk. But this is not always the case!

6. Dawn and dusk are often fruitful times to fish, especially when either coincides with a rising or high tide.

7. Keep a tight line on hooked fish; pull the rod upright and recover line in time with incoming waves (reel-in as waves come towards the shore), then the tide carries your fish to you. Don't strain too hard on the line, or the hook might rip from the fish's mouth – and lose the fish!

8. Once you've safely "beached" the hooked fish in shallow water, swing it ashore, or "tail" the fish; grab the fish's tail end and carry it ashore *after you're certain it's not a species with poisonous spines or stings or a nasty spur*!!! See Chapter 3; particularly the weevers, on page 61; sting ray, page 53, and spurdog, page 32. Be wary of conger eels – they may tail you!

9. A beach caster's rod rest gives YOU a rest, but should not be over employed. Bites are missed when a rod isn't held.

Safety Hints

* Don't get cut off by a rapidly rising tide.
* Before fishing isolated beaches, work out escape routes in event of mishap – no climbing cliffs! Clearly mark on your map quick escape routes to safety.
* Tie correct knots tightly. A heavy weight flying free from line you're casting could kill someone.
* Before casting, see there's nobody close behind.

Right methods and rigs for beach casting include:
Basic leger (see rig, page 114); simple paternoster (see rig, page 115); running paternoster (see rig, page 115); 2 hook

paternoster (see rig, page 116); 2 hook running leger (see rig, page 117); 2 boom paternoster (see rig, page 117); spinning (see trace, page 120) in deep water off steep shelving beach.

Tackle Notes (see also Ch 4)

Suitable rods: beach caster rods from 3.35 m (11 ft) to 3.96 m (13 ft) in length. A beach caster rod of 3.50 m (11½ ft) is ideal.

Suitable reels: fixed spool or multiplier.

Suitable line strength: main reel line from about 6.80 Kg (15 lbs) to 11.33 Kg (25 lbs) breaking strain. A main reel line of 9.07 Kg (20 lbs) breaking strain is a good strength for all-round beach casting.

When beach casting, to absorb the shock on main reel line of casting a heavy weight long distances, a shock *leader line* is tied to the reel line using the *leader knot* (see page 108). To be safe the shock leader line should be approximately 7 m (23 ft) in length and about *twice* the breaking strain strength of the reel line used. For example, when casting with a main reel line of 9.07 Kg (20 lbs) breaking strain, use the leader knot (see page 108) to tie 7 m (23 ft) of 18.14 Kg (40 lbs) breaking strain leader line to the main reel line.

The rig (weight and hook arrangement, see page 109) is tied to the leader line. Always attach the weight either direct to the leader line, or to line of the same breaking strain as the leader line (see rig designs, Ch 12).

TIP

Tie the leader line to main reel line and wind onto your reel at home, before setting out to beach cast.

Suitable weights: from about 85 g (3 oz) to 170 g (6 oz) depending on strength of current and the distance you wish to cast. A 142 g (5 oz) weight is normally adequate for long distance beach casting in strong currents.

9

PIER INTO YON DISTANCE

Walking on water takes practice; walking over water on a pier or jetty is easy; a marvellous cheating way to fish deep water – no long casts from the beach to worry about, simply stroll to the end of the pier or jetty and let down your line.

Yes, a pier is the easiest way to present your baited hook to fish swimming out there – in yon distance!

Piers and jetties attract fish. The weed-covered supports are home for many shellfish and shelter shoals of small fish from strong currents and waves. Holiday makers, boat trippers, pier cafes and restaurants – each pitches the odd unwanted sandwich, scraps and leftovers into waves lapping the supports. All scrumptious food for big fish!

Among fish you may expect to catch from piers and/or jetties, depending on locality, season and type of seabed (see Ch 3) are: bass, bream, coalfish, cod, conger eels, dabs, dogfish, flounders, garfish, mackerel, mullet, plaice, pollack, pouting, skates, whiting, wrasse etc.

Unfortunately, piers and jetties were not erected solely for sea anglers and few extend over prime fishing ground. However, the merits and sporting potential of particular piers and jetties are soon checked by referring to local tackle dealers, sea anglers; angling newspapers or magazines.

NOTE: Most of the following tips and hints apply to piers *and* jetties.

TIPS

1. Study the seabed beneath the pier or jetty at low tide. Look for patches of sand or sand/mud between rocks; dips, holes, hollows and gullies likely to be searched for trapped food particles by fish patrolling the rising tide. Notice their precise position in relation to clearly visible and memorable structures on the pier or jetty. Also look out for iron girders, concrete blocks and other obstacles which, when submerged on the high tide, might snag and snap your line. Check for signs of whirling currents round supports – fish queue beside these eddies for snatches at spinning food sucked into the vortex. Weed-covered rocks, posts and pier or jetty supporting piles may prove great places to fish.

2. The best times to fish from a pier are generally dawn, dusk and night (if permitted). Many fish are attracted by lights on open-all-night piers. Big fish not fascinated by the lights are drawn to shoals of fish dancing to the underwater disco

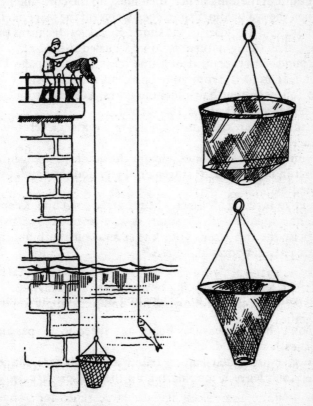

41. Drop net in use

effect of the lights, and big fish make a meal of the small fish! One and a half hours before high tide is a good time to begin fishing; your sport should peak at high tide. When high tide occurs at dawn or dusk – BONANZA! You'll catch more than your fair share of fish.

3. Where possible fish on the lower deck of a pier or near a boat landing stage. It's easier to land your fish from a lower level. There you may find a long handled landing net useful (especially on jetties). You'll need a sea angler's drop net to haul hooked heavy fish from the sea to a high pier deck (see sketch on page 95). A helpful friend saves the trouble of lowering the net yourself; manoeuvre your hooked fish over the mouth of the sunken net, then hoist up the cord and net.

4. When the sea's calm, fish in deep water off the pier end. In rough water, fish closer to the shore. Heavy swell churns the seabed, dislodging natural food and buried titbits.

5. Groundbait suspended in a fine mesh bag (see page 13) about 1.21 m (4 ft) from your hookbait attracts fish.

6. To foil persistent bait-pinching crabs, keep your bait at least 609 mm (2 ft) above the seabed.

7. Fishing your bait at roughly mid-water level often produces results.

8. If you're not getting bites, change the depth you're fishing the bait in 609 mm (2 ft) stages until you find the depth fish are feeding.

9. Hold your rod at all times – be prepared for a bite. Keep a tight line and reel-in as soon as you've hooked a fish; otherwise the fish wraps your line several turns around the pier or jetty supports and SNAP!

Do's And Dont's
1. Do learn the pier or jetty rules and regulations and abide by them.
2. Don't hook pleasure boats or speedboats passing underneath your rod.
3. Do give unwanted bait to fellow anglers before you go home; don't leave it mouldering on the pier or jetty deck.

Safety Hints
* Stay clear of the pier and lower decks in stormy seas. A high breaking wave may sweep you out to sea. It has happened!
* Don't push or shove other people.
* Never make an overhead cast from pier or jetty. The weight might snap loose and injure someone.

Right methods and rigs for pier and jetty fishing include:
Sliding float (see rig, page 111); basic leger (see rig, page 114) where the seabed is free from snags and crabs; simple paternoster (see rig, page 115); 2 hook paternoster (see rig, page 116); 3 hook paternoster (see rig, page 116); 2 boom paternoster (see rig, page 117).

From jetties in calm water a light float (see rig, page 111) may be used to catch mullet. When fishing from jetties and the lower decks of piers, spinning (see trace, page 120) frequently brings success; as does driftlining (see page 121) providing the current carries your line away from line-snagging obstacles.

Tackle Notes (see also Ch 4)
Suitable rods: strong rods, from 2.43 m (8 ft) to 3.50 m (11½ ft) in length.
Suitable reels: fixed spool or multiplier.
Suitable line strength: from about 4.53 Kg (10 lbs) to 6.80 Kg (15 lbs) breaking strain.
Suitable weights: any weight up to about 28 g (1 oz) depending on strength of current.

10

FISHING ON THE ROCKS

Fishing from rocks is an exciting and exhilarating experience. You might be on an easily accessible rock outcrop merely a few metres higher than the crashing waves, or 30 metres (100 ft) or move above the sea on top of a sheer rock face.

42. Huge cliffs and rocks on the coast of North Wales

Rocks are a rich source of fishes' natural food; provide protection from strong tidal currents; security from commercial trawlers, and handy holes and crevices for hiding from predators.

The seabed may be mainly sand with some rough ground and small rocks, or rough, rocky ground leading to a solid rock base rising massively above the waves and towering skywards.

Fish eat tiny creatures found in weed growing on rocks; fish also feed on crabs, fish fry, limpets, lugworms, mussels, prawns, razorfish, sandeels, shrimps etc. If you can safely approach the rock base at low tide, check for promising places to fish: clumps of weed and colonies of shellfish; patches of sand or sand/mud between rocks; hollows in the rocks; little caves and caverns; clefts, channels and lanes between rocks – well travelled fish "highways" leading from one feeding "hotspot" to another. Plan to intercept fish at these points with your hookbait. Fish closely hug the rock walls, picking at growths of weed and clinging creatures; playing hide-and-seek with friends and foes.

As the tide rises, so fish ride higher in the water, investigating every nook and cranny for recently deposited morsels of food. And keeping a hungry eye on smaller feeding fish are the BIG predators.

Among the fish that can be caught in season (see Ch 3) from rocks at various places round the coast are (depending on the nature of the seabed): bass, bream, coalfish, cod, conger eels, dabs, dogfish (bull huss), flounders, mackerel, plaice, pollack, pouting, whiting, wrasse, and sometimes rays, skates and tope.

Rock fishing may yield worthwhile catches and give good sport at any time of day; the best bags of fish are frequently caught on a rising tide near dawn, or as dusk approaches.

TIPS

1. Stay well back from the edge of rocks a few metres above the sea – for safety reasons *and* so the fish don't see you!

2. Groundbait suspended in a fine mesh bag (see page 13) or scattered loose attracts fish to your baited hook.

3. Choose a bait the fish will recognise as a natural food familiar to them round the rocks, and present that bait in a place and manner which seems normal and "natural" to the fish.

4. Keep your line tight to prevent it snagging and snapping on submerged rocks.

5. Reel-in line immediately a bite is indicated (see page 13). The hooked fish must be prevented from diving under or between rocks and severing your line.

6. You'll need a long handled landing net or drop net (see page 95) to lift fish from water a few metres below your rod tip. If you're fishing from a rock ledge many metres above the sea, you'll have to fish with extra strong line of at least 13.60 Kg (30 lbs) breaking strain so that you are able to haul your catch up the rock face.

Safety Hints

* Never go rock fishing alone.
* Wear walking or climbing boots; never rubber boots – they slip on wet rock.
* Carry a watch and make sure you know the times and heights of local tides. Stay well above rising tide waves.
* Keep back from the edge of rocks; avoid slippery weed covered sections; stick to safe positions you can quickly vacate if the weather and waves turn rough.
* NEVER run across rocks.
* Save up for a comfortable sea angler's flotation jacket and wear it – just in case!

Right methods and rigs for rock fishing include:
Sliding float (see rig, page 111); heavy float (see rig, page 113); expendable float (see rig, page 113); rotten bottom (see rig, page 119); spinning (see trace, page 120) for bass, mackerel and pollack; driftlining (see page 121); feathering (see page 121) for mackerel.

Tackle Notes: (see also Ch 4).
Suitable rods: strong rods, from 2.74 m (9 ft) to 3.65 m (12 ft) in length.

Suitable reels: fixed spool or multiplier.
Suitable line strength: from about 5.44 Kg (12 lbs) to 8.16 Kg (18 lbs) breaking strain. See also ***TIP*** number 6 on page 100.
Suitable weights: from about 14 g (½ oz) to 42 g (1½ oz) depending on the distance you wish to cast and strength of current.

11

ACE BOAT FISHING

Sea fishing from a dinghy accompanied by an *experienced* boat handler, or sea anglers' commercial charter boat, is an ace way to savour exciting angling over mysterious depths: there's the thrilling anticipation of turning up trumps and landing the BIG one!

Fish shoals often follow regular routes across the seabed to established feeding grounds, called MARKS. Known "marks" nearly always guarantee good results. Marks favoured by fish (see Ch 3) may be areas of sand, sand/mud, shell-grit, underwater rocks and reefs, deep holes, hollows, gullies, troughs or wrecks.

To learn boat fishing properly and locate the local "magic" fishing marks, put to sea with a professional charter boat skipper. He'll show you fish catching tricks taught him by fellow skippers and champion sea anglers. The most economical way to boat fish frequently is to join a sea angling club, and take advantage of the club's discount block booking scheme. Your club books a boat and skipper for a fishing expedition and off you go – all the joys and rewards of expertly supervised boat angling at low cost.

Inshore fishing
Sea angling from a boat within 4.82 Km (3 miles) of the shore is "inshore fishing". A dinghy (*close* inshore) or motor launch is normally adequate for this type of angling.

Inshore fishing near sand or sand/mud river estuaries produces fair-sized bass, dabs, flounders, mullet, plaice, thornback rays and occasionally turbot.

Rocky, rough inshore seabed is good hunting ground for coalfish, conger eels, dogfish (bull huss), pollack, pouting and wrasse.

Deep sea fishing

Once 4.82 Km (3 miles) or more away from the shore, you're deep sea fishing – regardless of the depth of water beneath the boat. A purpose-built sea-going vessel is essential for deep sea fishing.

Among the larger fish caught from deep sea marks are: big cod, coalfish, conger eels, halibut, ling, pollack, rays, skate, tope and turbot.

TIPS

Especially for supervised charter boat anglers

1. Don't drink too much home-brewed beer the night before your boat trip! Grab a restful night's sleep; dress in warm clothes and eat a light breakfast.

2. Pack a hearty lunch and flask of hot soup.

3. Take a spare pullover and waterproofs or a sea angler's flotation suit.

4. Tackle ought to include: a heavy, blunt instrument to kill fish for the family's cook; a sharp filleting knife; protective leather gloves for handling rough-skinned or spiny fish, and a sea angler's hook disgorger or artery forceps. A sea angler's long handled, large frame landing net helps board big fish!

5. And don't forget to take plenty of bait; a board on which to cut the bait; spare hooks and weights.

6. After fishing's finished, clean and tidy the boat. Leave everything "ship shape and Bristol fashion" and you'll be welcomed back, next time.

Safety Hints

Especially for supervised charter boat anglers

* Wear an inflatable life jacket (either your own or one supplied by the boat's skipper). A sea angler's flotation suit is a wise investment. Your life is worth the price!

* Never wear thigh boots in a boat. Should you fall overboard, they'll fill with water and sink you like a stone. Wear rubber soled walking boots or calf high rubber boots, and kick them off as soon as possible if you should go over the side.

Right methods and rigs for boat fishing include:
Sliding float (see rig, page 111); 2 hook running leger (see rig, page 117); 2 boom paternoster (see rig, page 117); boat leger (see rig, page 118); spinning (see trace, page 120); driftlining (see page 121); jigging (see page 122); trolling (see page 122); feathering (see page 121); even fly fishing inshore, using freshwater fly fishing tackle, techniques, and large artificial flies – for fish feeding on the surface, especially bass, mackerel and mullet.

Tackle Notes (see also Ch 4)
Suitable rods: powerful, stiff boat rods from 2.13 m (7 ft) to 2.43 m (8 ft) in length. Line class 9.07 Kg (20 lbs) or 13.60 Kg (30 lbs) – see page 66.
Suitable reel: multiplier.
Suitable line strength: from about 6.80 Kg (15 lbs) to 11.33 Kg (25 lbs) breaking strain for normal boat fishing with a 9.07 Kg (20 lbs) line class boat rod; about 11.33 Kg (25 lbs) to 15.87 Kg (35 lbs) breaking strain with a 13.60 Kg (30 lbs) line class boat rod, where particularly large and heavy fish are expected.
Suitable weights: from about 227 g (8 oz) to 0.90 Kg (2 lbs) depending on strength of current, depth and size of bait fished.

12
KNOTS, RIGS AND FISHING METHODS

Knots, rigs and sea fishing methods; some simple, others complicated, ingenious or plain weird!

Be warned: sea anglers DO become obsessed by the arrangement of hooks and weights at the end of line. I know sea anglers who spend more time designing and tying rigs than fishing!

Experienced anglers develop their own favourite super-successful rigs to suit specific localities and species of fish.

You'll soon devise your own winning rigs! And someone will sidle over to you, point inquisitively at your rig and say,

"What about the angle of the dangle on your doodum? What do you call it? How do you tie that!? Please show me."

TIP
To keep pace with the latest experiments and discoveries in "doodum" tackle rig construction, read sea angling newspapers and magazines.

KNOTS
Knots for sea anglers come into and pass out of fashion faster than ladies' hats. Learn a few good knots that work well for you; practise tying the knots to perfection, then stick with them until you need something different or stronger.

There's a right knot for every occasion, afloat and ashore. To be secure and solve *all* knotty problems, you can't do better than buy a copy of Geoffrey Budworth's masterly and comprehensive book, "The Knot Book", published in the same series as this book by *Elliot Right Way Books*.

Meanwhile, the following knots – properly tied – won't let you down.

TIP

To tighten knots fully; spit on them and pull the ends tight with angler's pliers. Saliva moistens the knot, easing the turns of line together firmly under pressure. When you trim the knot with pliers or scissors, leave "ends" of about 4 mm (⅛ inch).

Tucked half blood knot

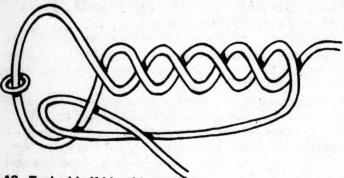

43. Tucked half blood knot

To tie line to a loop or any eyed item of tackle (hooks, swivels, split rings, weights etc.).

Universal or "grinner" knot

44. Universal or "grinner" knot

An extra-strong alternative to the tucked half blood knot (see above).

Blood loop

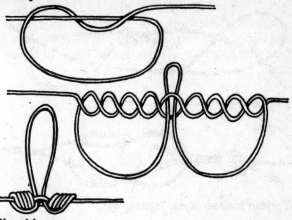

45. Blood loop

For tying a loop in main line. A short length of "stand off" line presenting the hook and bait is then tied to the blood loop. The short length of stand off line is commonly called a "snood" or "dropper" (see also page 110).

Double overhand loop knot

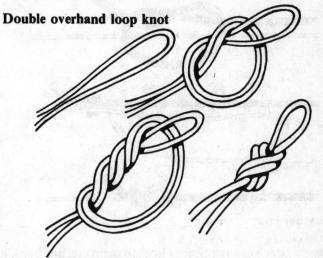

46. Double overhand loop knot

To tie a loop at the end of a length of line.

To join looped lines, traces, etc.

47. To join looped lines, traces, etc.

Simple, strong and effective way to join loop knotted lines, looped trace, etc.

Leader knot

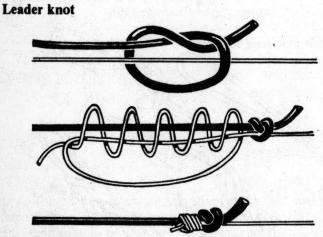

48. Leader knot

For tying beach casting "leader line" to main reel line (see Ch 8 and page 93).

Double grinner knot

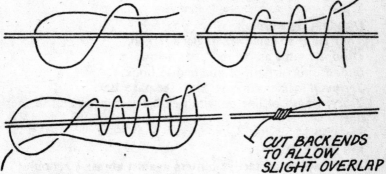

49. Double grinner knot

Strong knot to join 2 lines of equal or different breaking strain.

Stop knot

50. Stop knot

To stop a sliding float (see rig, page 111) at the required depth, and/or stop otherwise free-moving swivels, beads, weights etc. slipping unchecked along line.

RIGS

The term "rig" refers to the planned arrangement of float (if any), swivels and/or split rings, beads (if any), knots, weights, hooks etc. along the end section of your line – the part of your tackle set up that *catches fish*.

Right rigs to use for best catches of big fish of different species are listed in Ch 3 and in Chapters 7 to 11. However, the rigs shown on the following pages are but a few of the many "right rigs" that consistently bring success when properly fished.

QUESTION: "When is a right rig wrong?"
ANSWER: "When it doesn't catch fish!"

About rigs

Rigs can be made in comfort at home; wound on a small line winder frame, or carefully coiled, and stored tangle-free until wanted.

Ready-made rigs are marketed and available from your local specialist tackle dealer. Of course, they're more costly than home made rigs, but time-saving and convenient if you don't mind paying the price. They show how professionally tied rigs look.

Doodum rig words

Your guide to some sea angler's jargon.

Dropper: same as "snood", see below.

Snood: short length of line tied to hook.

Terminal tackle: same as "rig", see page 109.

Trace: length of line or wire tied between hook and main line.

RIG BITS

Beads: act as protective buffers against abrasive action of free sliding weights, swivels or split rings on knots tied in main line.

Leger stops: angler's plastic leger stops may be used on line in place of stop knots (see page 109) tied to line.

Split rings: strong and less expensive alternative to swivels (see below) for attaching line and pieces of tackle to line. However, unlike swivels, split rings don't help prevent kinks, twists or tangles in line.

Swivels: "swivelling" action of rotating swivel eyes prevents twists and kinks in line and helps stop tangles! Also an easy and efficient way of joining lengths of line and/or linking weights to line.

To make the rigs illustrated in this book, you may choose to buy swivels and/or split rings, beads and leger stops from your tackle dealer, or put the rigs together using only simple knots and save money. They're *your* rigs!

RIG NOTES
The object of any rig is to present hookbait in a "natural" way to the species of fish you're hunting, without alarming the fish or making them suspicious.

If your rig fools fish into seizing the bait, it's a winning rig. Sketch your best fish-catching rig designs in an exercise book or "log" book.

Think about the place on or near the seabed, and/or the depth you want to present your hookbait to particular fish (refer to Ch 3). Take a close look at rig designs and decide which one is more likely to catch fish. Then construct the rig.

Make a few different rigs at home and act the part of a wily big fish – see how the rigs look through your pretend fish's eye. Tug the hook and feel the resistance fish will be aware of as they examine the bait. *Think* about the rig *before* you use it.

The battle of wits with big fish is won at home in the comfy chair, before you go fishing!

TIPS
1. Keep rigs simple.
2. After use, check rigs for signs of damage – cuts, nicks, splits etc. and line strain (limpness). A damaged or strained rig loses fish! Replace parts where necessary. Expert sea anglers regularly re-tie rigs with new line.

Light float rig
Use a slim float and small freshwater fishing weights – enough to sink (cock) the float so only its tip shows clearly above the water. Adjust to present your baited hook at the depth you expect fish to be feeding (see Ch 3). Re-adjust when necessary to allow for rise and fall of tide etc.

Sliding float rig
Use a narrow float. Tie a stop knot (see page 109) onto the main line at the point where you want the float to stop. Re-

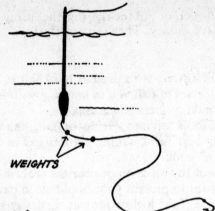

WEIGHTS

51. Light float rig

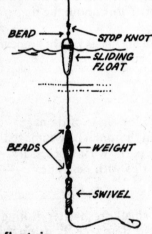

BEAD →   ← STOP KNOT

          ← SLIDING
               FLOAT

BEADS <   ← WEIGHT

                    ← SWIVEL

52. Sliding float rig

adjust when necessary to allow for rise and fall of tide etc. A "ball" or "barrel" shaped weight is ideal; attach the smallest weight required to cast the distance you want to achieve, and hold your bait against prevailing current(s) at the depth you expect fish to be feeding (see Ch 3). The distance between hook and swivel is variable, but should be at least 304 mm (1 ft).

Heavy float rig

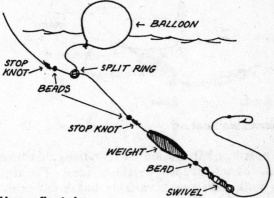

53. Heavy float rig

For float fishing large, "heavy" baits for big fish in deep water over rough or rocky ground where costly losses of conventional floats are probable, due to snagged and broken line. This rig also keeps most of the line below the water off sharp seabed rocks, if you decide to present your hookbait lying on the bottom. Remember to make periodic changes in the depth setting (when necessary) to allow for rise and fall of tide. Small, bright coloured balloons, of the type which would be around 102 mm (4 inches) fully inflated, may be partially inflated to give lower resistance to a fish swimming away with the hookbait. Use a small split ring that won't pass over the bead and stop knot/leger stop. A "ball" or "barrel" shaped weight is ideal. The distance between hook and swivel is variable, but should be at least 304 mm (1 ft).

Expendable float rig
To fish over rough or rocky ground where costly float losses are probable. A chunk of polystyrene tile or packaging is usable, as are sealed and painted small plastic bottles, scraps

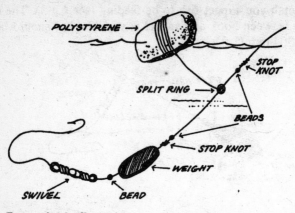

54. Expendable float rig

of cork board or balsa wood etc. Anything that floats! A "ball" or "barrel" shaped weight is ideal. The distance between hook and swivel is variable, but should be at least 304 mm (1 ft). Adjust depth setting of the "float" (if necessary) to allow for rise and fall of tide.

Basic leger rig

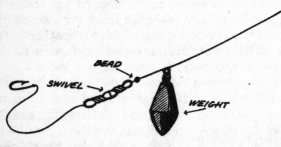

55. Basic leger rig

To lay hookbait on the seabed. The distance between hook and swivel is variable, but should be at least 304 mm (1 ft). Because your line is free to pass through the weight's "eye", shy or suspicious fish can tug the bait without immediately feeling resistance.

Simple paternoster rig

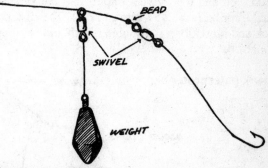

BEAD

SPLIT RING →

← SWIVEL

WEIGHT

56. Simple paternoster rig

To present your bait above the seabed, moving with the current. The distance between weight and split ring is variable, but should be at least 304 mm (1 ft). The distance between hook and swivel (free running on main line) is variable, but should be at least 152 mm (6 inches).

Running paternoster rig

BEAD

SWIVEL

WEIGHT

57. Running paternoster rig

To offer your hookbait anchored above the seabed, and permit fish to take the bait without immediately feeling resistance from the weight. The distance between hook and swivel is variable, but should be at least 152 mm (6 inches). The distance between weight and swivel on connecting line is variable, but should normally be about 609 mm (2 ft).

2 hook paternoster rig

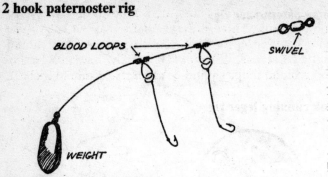

58. 2 hook paternoster rig

To present 2 baited hooks above the seabed. Two different hookbaits may be used if you wish. Some beach casting (see Ch 8) anglers clip a small split ring onto the weight's "eye" and tie line to the split ring, thereby reducing seabed wear and tear on the knot. Alternatively, the line can be tied direct to the weight. 3 way swivels may be used in place of the blood loops. The distances between weight, 1st blood loop and 2nd blood loop and top swivel/or split ring, are variable but each should normally be 457 mm (1½ ft). The distance between hook and blood loop is variable but should be about 203 mm (8 inches).

3 hook paternoster rig

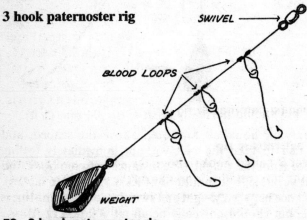

59. 3 hook paternoster rig

To present three hooks and baits above the seabed at different depths. Three different baits may be used. The distance between each blood loop is variable, but should normally be at least 457 mm (1½ ft). The lines connecting hooks to blood loops should be at least 203 mm (8 inches).

2 hook running leger rig

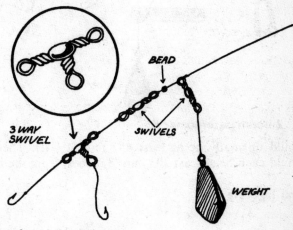

60. 2 hook running leger rig

To present 2 hookbaits on or very near the seabed. Two different baits may be fished. The distance between hooks and 3 way swivel is variable, but should be at least 203 mm (8 inches). To fish the bait just above the seabed, attach the weight to a swivel on the main line by a line about 1 m (3 ft) long; or to lay the bait on the seabed, fit the weight direct to the main line. The distance between 3 way swivel and bead is variable, but should normally be at least 304 mm (1 ft).

2 boom paternoster rig

To present 2 baited hooks above the seabed, and moving freely in the current. Plastic booms rid the possibility of lines tangling and encourage vigorous movement of the baits in a current. Two different baits may be fished. The distance between weight and boom is variable, but each spacing

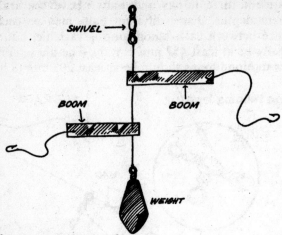

61. 2 boom paternoster rig

should normally be at least 457 mm (1½ ft). The hooks should each be at least 203 mm (8 inches) from the booms.

Boat leger rig

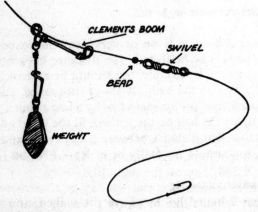

62. Boat leger rig

Simple and effective leger rig for boat anglers. The distance between hook and swivel is variable, but should normally be about 1m (3 ft). Your bait is presented on the seabed; line is free to move through the boom without jarring against the weight to alarm a bait-biting fish.

Rotten bottom rigs

63. Rotten bottom rig

For use when fishing over reefs or rocks, where you're prepared to lose a trapped weight, but reluctant also to lose swivels, hooks and long lengths of line. If your weight is inextricably caught among rocks, steady pressure on your line by pulling with gloved hands (don't strain your rod) snaps the weaker "light" line attaching weight to main line. The lighter line should be ABOUT half the breaking strain of the main line. The distance between weight and swivel is variable, but should normally be at least 203 mm (8 inches). The hook ought to be a minimum of 152 mm (6 inches) from swivel or blood loop on the main line.

Economical rotten bottom rigs can be constructed with expendable weights like bolts, nuts, stones with naturally worn holes etc. (see fig 63B above).

DON'T make sweeping overhead casts from the shore with a rotten bottom rig. The weight could break loose and injure someone!

Spinning trace

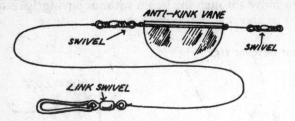

64. Spinning trace

To spin a bait, usually an aritifical lure, simply cast your line and then reel-in. Raise and lower your rod tip; move the rod tip from side to side, and vary your reeling-in speed. These actions make the spinning bait/lure come "alive" to interested fish. The link swivel snaps onto the swivel-eye on lures; enabling fast change of lures when required. However, the trace line can be tied direct to the lure's swivel-eye or an eyed hook. The anti-kink vane helps prevent kinks, twists and tangles in line. A special anti-kink weight may be attached to the trace or main line in addition to, or instead of, the anti-kink vane. The attachment of an anti-kink weight gives potential for casting longer distances; sinks the bait/lure deeper in the water and slows the rate of "spin". The distance between link swivel and anti-kink vane is variable, but should normally be about 762 mm (2½ ft) to 1.52 m (5 ft) depending on the size of bait/lure you're using and depth of water you're spinning.

Wire trace

For attaching to line when hunting fish with strong jaws and sharp, line-cutting teeth. Angler's trace wire is marketed in strengths ranging from 4.53 Kg (10 lbs) breaking strain to over 91 Kg (200 lbs) breaking strain. Special ready-assembled wire traces and hooks suitable for conger eels, halibut, ling, skate and tope are stocked by specialist tackle dealers, or you can make your own. You'll need angler's crimping pliers to "crimp" tight the securing metal crimps or "ferrules" (see fig 65). The length of wire traces is variable,

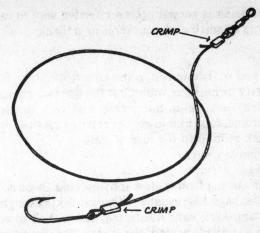

65. Wire trace

but should normally be at least 457 mm (1½ ft). One metre
(3 ft) is a popular minimum length. For big fish use a wire
trace of at least 36.28 Kg (80 lbs) breaking strain.

MORE USEFUL METHODS

Driftlining
From shore or anchored boat; simply cast your line and let it
"drift" with the current. The depth your bait is presented to
fish depends on: a) length of line released from your reel; b)
strength of current; and c) weight of bait and amount of
additional weight (if any) attached to the line.

Feathering
Fishing a hook or series of hooks wrapped around with
feathers (real or imitation) and attached to your line.
Commercially marketed feathering traces are available from
sea angling tackle dealers. Once you see how they're put
together, you can make your own!

The feathers, imitating a small shoal of tiny fish, may be
trailed behind a boat, or cast out on line (which can be
weighted) from pier, jetty, harbour wall or rock outcrop, and
retrieved in a jerky manner to excite and attract hungry fish.

Feathering is sometimes an effective way to catch large numbers of small cod; mackerel or pollack.

Jigging

A method of fishing bait, often an artificial lure, from boat, pier, jetty or harbour wall. Cast the line (which may also be weighted) and reel-in line jerkily and very slowly. As you recover line, raise and lower the rod tip to give a "jigged" rise and sink motion to the lure or bait.

Trolling

Style of fishing from a slow moving boat. A basic spinning trace (see page 120) usually with an anti-kink weight in place of the anti-kink vane illustrated, is attached to your main line and trailed behind the boat. The depth your bait (commonly an artificial lure) is presented to fish depends on: a) speed of the boat and length of line released – normally about 50 m (55 yds); and b) amount of weight attached to the line.

13

COOK YOUR CATCH

Eat delicious meals prepared from freshly-caught fish and know the highly nutritious flesh, low in fat; protein and vitamin rich, is completely free of the chemical additives found in some commercially marketed fish.

Bumper catches of fish are easily cleaned and filleted or cut into chunky cutlets and frozen sea-fresh in your freezer. Frozen fresh fish stays in excellent condition for at least 3 months.

Many exciting, mouth-watering fish dish recipes are widely available to enthusiastic chefs. The liberal use of inexpensive home made wine, beer or cider bestows a new zest to appetizing fish cookery.

Fish is quickly digested, and, according to grandma, "good for the brain."

By the sea
Fish you decide to keep for cooking should be killed straight away. To kill a fish, strike it firmly across the back of its head with a heavy object. Conger eels are a special case, see page 29. Store the dead fish in a shady place out of sun and wind.

Gut fish as soon as convenient after killing them; simply slit open the stomach and remove insides. The liver plus any roe (eggs) may be kept and cooked.

Don't leave slippery fish guts lying about. Either put the guts in a plastic bag or covered container for use later the same day as groundbait, or throw the guts into the sea as a gift to the fish.

Cut off and dispose of spines or spurs (see spurdog, page 32). Removing the head from large fish is optional, but does save carrying extra weight on the journey home. Some chefs prefer to cook fish with the head left on. Rinse the gutted fish in salt water to get rid of blood and torn skin tissue.

At home

Scrape off fish scales in warm water. Remove fins and tail and skin (if appropriate) with a sharp knife. Trim the fish flesh into slim fillets or slice into chunky cutlets.

FISH FOR THE FREEZER MUST BE FROZEN WITHIN 24 HOURS OF BEING CAUGHT.

Portions

227 g (½ lb) of fish per person satisfies the healthiest appetites!

TIP

Most of the flesh on rays and skates is found on the wings. Conger eels taste superb cooked and served in their skins.

Popular ways to cook fish

Baked fish: bass, cod, conger eels (skinning optional), dogfish, gurnard, halibut, john dory, ling, mackerel, rays (cut off and cook skinned wings only); skates (cut off and cook skinned wings only); soles (skinned), turbot, whiting.

Boiled or stewed fish: cod, conger eels (skinning optional), halibut, john dory, mackerel, skates (cut off and cook skinned wings only); soles (skinned), turbot.

Casseroled fish: angler fish, brill, coalfish, cod, conger eels (skinning optional), dogfish, halibut, ling, pollack turbot.

Fried fish: bream, coalfish, cod, dabs, dogfish, flounders, garfish, halibut, john dory, ling, mackerel, plaice, pollack, rays (cut off and cook skinned wings only); skates (cut off and cook skinned wings only); soles (skinned), whiting.

Grilled fish: bass, bream, cod, conger eels (skinning optional), dabs, dogfish, halibut, john dory, ling, mackerel, plaice, rays (cut off and cook skinned wings only); skates (cut off and cook skinned wings only); soles (skinned), tope.

BON APPÉTIT!

INDEX

A

Admiralty charts 11
Angler fish, **main article** 16
Artery forceps 68
Artificial baits 82, 83

B

Baits 71 *et seq.*
Ballan wrasse, **main article** 64
"Balls" 67
Basic leger rig 114
Bass, **main article** 17
Beachcasting 89 *et seq.*, distance 90,
  rods 66, style 89, 90
Beads 110
Bird behaviour 11
Blood loop knot 107
Boat fishing 102 *et seq.*, leger rig
  118, rods 66
"Bombs" 67
Breakwaters 91
Bream: black, **main article** 19; red,
  main article 21
Brill, **main article** 22
Bull huss, **main article** 30/32

C

Clams as bait 73
Clothing 84
Coalfish, **main article** 23
Cockles as bait 73
Cod, **main article** 25
Coelacanth 7
Common limpets as bait 76
Common skate, **main article** 56
Conger eel, **main article** 26
Cooking fish 123 *et seq.*
Crabs as bait 73, 78
Cuckoo wrasse, **main article** 64

D

Dab, **main article** 29
Dangerous fish: angler fish 16;
  bream, red 21; bull huss 33;
  conger eel 26, 29; dogfish, lesser
  spotted 33; garfish 36; gurnard 38;
  halibut 41; john dory 43; ling 44;
  small-eyed ray 54; spurdog 33;
  sting ray 54; thornback ray 54;
  tope 58; weever, greater 61;
  weever, lesser 62; whiting 63
Deep sea fishing 103
Detecting bites 13
Dogfish: **main article** 30, lesser
  spotted 32
Double grinner knot 109
Double overhand loop knot 107
Driftlining 121
Drop net 88, 95
"Dropper" 107, 110

E

Earthworms as bait 74, 77
Ebb tide 10
Eel, conger, **main article** 26
Emergency survival kit 84
Estuaries 86 *et seq.*, mud danger 87
Expendable float rig 113

F

Feathering 121
Filling reels with line 67
First aid kit 85
Fish: as bait 74, behaviour 11, as
  food 7
Fishing after dark 70
Fixed spool reels 67
Flood tide 10
Flounder: **main article** 34, in
  freshwater 35, resemblance to
  plaice 49
Flying fish, related to garfish 36
Freezing fish 124

G

Garfish, **main article** 36
Golden grey mullet 47
Greater weever, **main article** 61
Grey mullet 47
"Grinner" knot 106
Groundbaiting 13, 87, 96, 99
Gurnard: **main article** 38, grey 38,
  red 38, yellow 38
Gutting fish 123

H

Haddock, **main article** 39
Halibut, **main article** 40
Harbours 87 *et seq.*
Headlamp 70

Heavy float rig 113
Hermit crabs as bait 74, 78
Hooks: disgorger 68, sizes 67, 68
"Huss" 33

I
Inshore fishing 102

J
Jigging 122
John dory, **main article** 42

K
Killing a fish 123
Knots 105 *et seq.*
"Kraken" 8

L
Landing net 88
Large fish 7
Lask 75, 76
Leader knot 108
Leger stops 110
Lesser weever 62
"Leviathan" 8
Light float rig 111, 112
Limpets as bait 76
Lines 67, for beach casting 93,
    for boat fishing 104, for estuary
    and harbour fishing 88, for pier
    fishing 97, for rock fishing 101
Ling, **main article** 44
Lobworms as bait 74
Local knowledge 9
Lugworms as bait 77, 78

M
Mackerel, **main article** 45
"Marks" 102
Mullet: thick-lipped, **main
    article** 46, golden grey 47;
    grey 47; thin-lipped 46
Multiplier reels 67
Mussels as bait 79

N
Neap tide 10

P
Paternosters 115 *et seq.*
"Pears" 67
Pirks 82, 83
Plaice, **main article** 49
Pollack, **main article** 50

Pouting, **main article** 52
Prawns as bait 77, 80
Preserved baits 82

R
Ragworms as bait 77, 80, 81
Ray: sting, **main article** 53;
    small-eyed 54; thornback,
    main article 54
Razorfish as bait 80
Reel lubricant 68
Reels 67, for beach casting 93,
    for boat fishing 104, for estuary
    and harbour fishing 88, for
    pier fishing 97, for rock fishing
    101
Rigs 109 *et seq.*
Rock salmon 33.
Rod and reel matching 67
Rod rest 92
Rods 66, for beach casting 93,
    for boat fishing 104, for estuary
    and harbour fishing 88, for
    pier fishing 96, for rock fishing
    100
Rotten bottom rigs 119
Running paternoster rig 115

S
Safety 84 *et seq.*, 100, 103
Saltwater corrosion 69
Sandeels: as artificial lures 83,
    as bait 77, 81
Scarcity of haddock 39, 40
Shark, tope as member of family
    58
Simple paternoster rig 115
"Sinkers" 67
Skate, common, **main article** 56
Slack water 10
Sliding float rig 111, 112
Slipper limpets as bait 76
Small-eyed ray 54
Smoothhound, **main article** 30
"Snood" 107, 110
Sole, **main article** 57
Spinners 82, 83
Spinning trace 120
Split rings 110
Spoons 82, 83
Spring tides 10
Spurdog, **main article** 30/32
Squid as bait 78
St. Peter's fish 43

Starry smoothhound, **main article** 30

Sting ray, **main article** 53

Stop knot 109

Swivels 110

T

Tackle: quality of 66 *et seq.*, shops 9, tips 69

Terminal tackle 110

Thick-lipped mullet, **main article** 46

Thin-lipped mullet, 46

Thornback ray, **main article** 54

3 hook paternoster rig 116

Tidal constants 10

Tides 9, in estuaries 86, 87

Tope: **main article** 58, member of shark family 58, smoothhound confused with 31

"Torpedoes" 67

Trace 110, 120 *et seq.*

Trolling 122

Tubfish 38

Tucked half blood knot 106

Turbot, **main article** 59

2 boom paternoster rig 117

2 hook: paternoster rig 116, running leger rig 117

U

Universal knot 106

W

Weever: greater, **main article** 61; lesser 62

Weights 67, for beach casting 92, 93, for boat fishing 104, for estuary and harbour fishing 88, for pier fishing 97, for rock fishing 101

Whiting, **main article** 62

Wire trace 120

Wrasse, **main article** 64

Wrecks 11

Other Right Way *titles for the Fisherman*

THE KNOT BOOK

Geoffrey Budworth has selected over 100 knots from his 45 years' practical knotting experience. He advises the National Maritime Museum, Greenwich, is a founder member of the International Guild of Knot-Tyers and created the knot identification method adopted by police forensic scientists. Let him teach you how to tie the right knot - secure and strong enough for the job.

Other fishing titles by Ian Ball

BEGIN FISHING THE RIGHT WAY

Teaches you how to catch big fish from both freshwater and sea. With descriptions of the plants and creatures you will see while fishing and hints on how to develop your angling skills, this book shows how, on a modest budget, all of us can enjoy this great outdoor sport.

SECRETS OF FLY-FISHING FOR TROUT

Beginning with a look at the fascinating watery world of the trout and the intriguing life-cycles of natural flies, Ian Ball teaches the best techniques to enable you to catch bumper bags of big trout.

FRESHWATER FISHING PROPERLY EXPLAINED

Of value to beginner and experienced angler, this marvellous book is packed with facts, tips and hints to help you catch more and bigger fish!

All uniform with this book

If you would like an up-to-date list of all *Right Way* titles currently available, send a stamped self-addressed envelope to:
ELLIOT RIGHT WAY BOOKS, BRIGHTON ROAD,
LOWER KINGSWOOD, TADWORTH, SURREY KT20 6TD, U.K.
or visit our web site at www.right-way.co.uk